1,000,000 Books

are available to read at

Forgotten Books

www.ForgottenBooks.com

Read online
Download PDF
Purchase in print

ISBN 978-1-332-60873-7
PIBN 10177355

This book is a reproduction of an important historical work. Forgotten Books uses state-of-the-art technology to digitally reconstruct the work, preserving the original format whilst repairing imperfections present in the aged copy. In rare cases, an imperfection in the original, such as a blemish or missing page, may be replicated in our edition. We do, however, repair the vast majority of imperfections successfully; any imperfections that remain are intentionally left to preserve the state of such historical works.

Forgotten Books is a registered trademark of FB &c Ltd.
Copyright © 2018 FB &c Ltd.
FB &c Ltd, Dalton House, 60 Windsor Avenue, London, SW19 2RR.
Company number 08720141. Registered in England and Wales.

For support please visit www.forgottenbooks.com

1 MONTH OF FREE READING

at www.ForgottenBooks.com

By purchasing this book you are eligible for one month membership to ForgottenBooks.com, giving you unlimited access to our entire collection of over 1,000,000 titles via our web site and mobile apps.

To claim your free month visit: www.forgottenbooks.com/free177355

* Offer is valid for 45 days from date of purchase. Terms and conditions apply.

English
Français
Deutsche
Italiano
Español
Português

www.forgottenbooks.com

Mythology Photography **Fiction**
Fishing Christianity **Art** Cooking
Essays Buddhism Freemasonry
Medicine **Biology** Music **Ancient Egypt** Evolution Carpentry Physics
Dance Geology **Mathematics** Fitness
Shakespeare **Folklore** Yoga Marketing
Confidence Immortality Biographies
Poetry **Psychology** Witchcraft
Electronics Chemistry History **Law**
Accounting **Philosophy** Anthropology
Alchemy Drama Quantum Mechanics
Atheism Sexual Health **Ancient History**
Entrepreneurship Languages Sport
Paleontology Needlework Islam
Metaphysics Investment Archaeology
Parenting Statistics Criminology
Motivational

AKUNIN'S WRITINGS

BY

GUY A. ALDRED.

MODERN PUBLISHERS, INDORE.
Available at—
LIBERTARIAN BOOK HOUSE,
Arya Bhavan, Sandhurst Road,
BOMBAY, 4.

PRICE RS. 2/-

Published by:—
MODERN PUBLISHERS,
INDORE CITY.

IMPORTANT NOTICE.

Books and Pamphlets published by the Modern Publishers of Indore and those of other Publishers that are sold by Libertarian Book House, are sold on the condition that they will be taken back if not approved within a week from the sale date and full amount of the cost minus 5% will be refunded to the purchaser if the books returned are in good condition and are not spoiled. As we are confident that our books give full value for the money so there will be very few returns.

Please take advantage of this offer and ask for the list of the books which will be supplied free anywhere in India.

MANAGER,
THE LIBERTARIAN BOOK HOUSE.

Printed by:—
C. M. SHAH,
MODERN PRINTERY LTD.,
INDORE CITY.

MUTUAL BANKING

BY GREENE.

SOME OF THE CONTENTS.

Value, Currency, The Disadvantages of a Specie Currency.

The Business of Banking.

Bills of Exchange.

The rate of Interest, Advantages of Mutual Banking.

Mutual money Generally Competent to Force its own Way

Into General Circulation. The Measure of Value.

The Regulator of value.

The Provincial Land Bank.

Money, Advantage of a Mutual Currency.

Credit, Legitimate Credit.

Mutual Credit Mutual Bank in Operation,

Price Rs. 1-4-0.

Available at:—

LIBERTARIAN BOOK HOUSE,
ARYA BHAVAN, SANDHURST ROAD.
BOMBAY, 4.

OR

MODERN PUBLISHERS, INDORE CITY.

RISE & FALL OF THE COMINTERN
by K. Tilak

Preface by Ajit Roy.   Price: Rs. 4/-

ONLY AVAILABLE HISTORY OF THE COMMUNIST INTERNATIONAL

THIS VOLUME ANSWERS SUCH QUESTIONS AS:

* Why did the German CP retreat in 1923?
* Who sabotaged the Chinese Revolution (1925-27)?
* What was the Left Opposition?
* What is "bureaucratic centrism"?
* Who helped Hitler to power?
* How did Fascism consolidate itself?
* What is "Popular Frontism"?
* Is the Soviet Union a Workers' State?
* Why defend the Soviet Union?
* Why the Fourth International?

—AND SHOWS THE BOLSHEVIK ROAD

to the

PROLETARIAN CONQUEST OF POWER

* * * *

ORDER FROM YOUR LOCAL BOOKSTALL OR WRITE TO:-

SPARK SYNDICATE
500, 16TH ROAD, BOMBAY, 21.

BAKUNIN'S WRITINGS

FORWARD.

Herewith is a collection of essays by Michael Bakunin. For the translations I am indebted to my comrade James Hainsy, who still lives in Glasgow, and remains a loyal disciple of Proudhon, the pioneer of Anarchist thought, "Crastinus", which was the nom-de-plume of Silvioc Coris, the famous friend of Malalesta, and a refugee long settled in London, whom I met some time back on a visit to London, and found him as fearless and as intrepid as ever, despite his years, Karl Laber, a famous German refugee and one of the main characters in booksellers London, still living his heretic life in the midst of Bohemian London; and Fred Cohen, now lost in South Africa, and probably retired from all activity.

"The workers and The Sphinx" is an address delivered by Bakunin in 1867, under the title of "The International." This speech naturally falls into two sections. The second portion is entitled in this collection, "Solidarity in Liberty".

"The policy of the Council" was published in "Egalite" in 1869. Bakunin stresses the necessity of membership of the First International. To Bakunin, of course, the First International was just The International. Since Bakunin pioneered the idea of Council organisation, I have substituted the word "Council" for "International", and have made one or two slight verbal alterations consistent with that change. The essay remains Bakunin's in thought and style, except for the "Council" substitution. Conditions make this change imperative and enhance the utility of the essay. To-day there is no International. No International is possible until Social Revolution becomes a household word in every country. That means a Renaissance in Britain, a New Britain, with groupings for freedom and struggle and rebirth throughout the country. In order that this slight and useful change may not do Bakunin an injustice, the "International" is preserved and no alteration made in "the policy of the International".

For "the Red Association' I have substituted "Council of Action" for "International', and also "world" for "Europe", where-ever Bakunin speaks of the organisation and struggle of the workers against Capital.

"The Class War", written in 1870, requires a word of explanations to the present reader. In February, 1848, the workers of Paris declared for a "Social Republic". In June, 1848, the bourgeois Republicans took State power and assassinated the workers' movement. Louis Bonapartist coup d'etat of December, 1851, when the bourgeois Republicans were persecuted and exiled, was a natural consequence of the parliamentary debacle of June, 1848. Marx has treated the matter ably in his **18th Brumaire.** Bakunin treats the matter from the same angle as Marx, and shows, as does Marx, that parliamentarism ends in Empire. Fascism is the logic of parliamentarism, the last word of the Joint Stock Republic.

Hitlerism is foreshadowed in Bakunin's "German Crisis", extracted from his "Letters to a Frenchman" written at

Locarno September 3rd. to 9th., 1870. He attacks the program adopted by the German Labour Unions at Nuremberg 1868, and readopted at Eisenach on August 7th, 1870. The third article of the Nuremberg program, and the fourth of the Eisenach, declared that political liberty was the indispensable preliminary condition to the economical liberation of the labouring classes." Bakunin saw in this item the inevitable reformist betrayal of the workers through politics. Time has justified his conclusion.

"The Commune, the Church and the State" is taken from the "Paris Commune and the State Idea" published in 1871. Bakunin does not differ from Marx's analysis of the Commune. Both were upholders of the Commune. Bakunin is jealous that the heroism of the communards should be respected and he is against the dictatorship idea. He saw the English and American socialists retreating to parliamentary reformism while loudly adopting the authoritarian communist ideas of the German school. His indignation caused him, on one occasion, to declare that he was not a communist. Actually he believed that the dictatorship spelt the defeat of communism. This essay, eulogising the libertarian, federal, ideas of Proudhon, will repay study. It is critical, practical and useful.

"God or Labour" is taken from Bakunin's preface to his pamphlet refuting Mazzini's theistic idealism, published in 1871. After over sixty years the vibrating audacity of Bakunin's thoughts, their penetrating inwardness and their generosity are as alive as ever.

The last work to be included is "God and the State". Noted for the singular vigour of it's logic this essay belongs to the second part of "The Knoutogerman Empire". It is only a fragment, part of an ambitious piece of work, interrupted by the author's journey to Jura during the closing days of the Paris Commune. Bakunin intended to charge the marxists with having taken as a basis of of their materialistic conception of history a principle which is eminently true from a relative point of view and reduced it to a Sophism. They made it entirely false by treating it as an absolute abstract principle. He never completed this work. "My life itself is a fragment," was his excuse for not completing his writings.

This apology is recalled by Carlo Cafiero and Elisee Reclus in their preface to the first French edition published at Geneva in 1882. "Composed in the same manner as most of Bakunin's other writings, it has the same literary fault, lack of proportion," is their very just comment.

Cafiero and Reclus altered the text slightly in order to make Bakunin's French look more smooth and literary. Their copyist often misread his handwriting.

Benjamin R. Tucker translated from their edition, which became the basis of the English version down to 1910. M. Nettlau, embodying Tuker's rendering to the fullest possible extent, compared it with the text of the original manuscript of Bakunin and amended wherever necessary. Nettlau included also the variant, which puzzled the editor of the 1882 edition, and is included here under the "critical Addenda (b)."

I found that "God and the State," despite its powerful declamation, made tiresome reading because of

Bakunin's love of repeating the same words, phrases, and almost whole paragraphs over and over again. After careful consideration, I determined to remedy partly this defect by editing the writing, and deleting some of this repetition. I regard a man's work from the standpoint of its utility, not its sanctity. I cannot see the sense of "choking" the reader off thinking by tiring him from sheer love of putting the same thing down a dozen time because that was Bakunin's unfortunate way, especially when it represented not a deliberate style, but a pure carelessness of execution As little deletion as possible has been made, almost all Bakunin's phrases have been saved, and no single thought has been omitted.

I have left out as unnecessary the paragraph in which Bakunin develops his hatred of Germany and eulogy of Italy The Latin spirit of Mussolini and the German spirit of Hitler meet in a common enmity to the commonweal of mankind. Stars (esterics) in the text indicate that Bakunin's manuscript was missing.

The opinion, I entertain, that Bakunin's work is not really opposed to Marx's is too well known to need repetition. In his point of difference with Marxism my sympathies are with Bakunin. As pioneers, Marx and Bakunin served, with unequal distinction but with equal abandon, the cause we Communists have at heart. If we are to be told that Stalinism is the logic of Marxism then my stand is with Bakunin against the monster. Does this stand for Stalin. It is not clear. He pioneered Sovietism, but deelared that the establishment of revolutionary terror was opposed to revolutionary progress.

" The guillotine, " he cries, " has never killed reaction, but only given it a new lease of life. The Revolution is neither vindictive nor blood-thirsty. It demands only the internment of its enemies as a simple measure of precaution. "

"We cannot admit," he says again, " even as a revolutionary transition, a so-called revolutionary dictatorship, because when the revolution becomes concentrated in the hands of some individuals it becomes inevitably and immediately reaction. "

Glasgow November 24, 1947.   **Guy A. Aldred**

WHERE I STAND

By
Michael Bakunin

I AM a passionate seeker after truth (and no less embittered enemy of evil doing fictions) which the *party of order,* this official, privileged and interested representative of all the past and present religions, metaphysical, political, juridical and "social" atrociousness claim to employ even to-day only to make the world stupid and enslave it. I am a fanatical lover of truth and freedom which I consider the only surroundings in which intelligence, consciousness and happiness develop and increase.

I do not mean the completely formal freedom which the State imposes, judges and regulates, this eternal lie which in reality consists always of the privileges of a few based upon the slavery of all—not even the individualist's, egotistical, narrow and fictitious freedom which the school of J. J. Rousseau and all other system of property moralists, middle class bourgeoisism and liberalism recommend—according to which the socalled rights of individuals which the State "represents" has the limit in the right of all, whereby the rights of every individual are necessarily, always reduced to nil. No, I consider only that as freedom worthy and real as its name should imply, which consists in the complete development of all material, intellectual and spiritual powers which are in a potential state in everyone, the freedom which knows no other limits than those prescribed by the laws of our own nature, so that there be really no limits—for these laws are not enforced upon us by external legislators who are around and over us, these laws are innate in us, clinging to us and form the real basis of our material, intellectual and moral being; instead of therefore seeing in them a limitation, we must look upon them as the real condition and the actual cause of our freedom.

Unconditional Freedom

I mean that freedom of the individual which, instead of stopping far from the freedom of others as before a frontier, sees on the contrary the cementing and the expansion into the infinity of its own free will, the *unlimited freedom of the individual through the freedom* of all; freedom through solidarity, freedom in equality; the freedom which triumphs over brute force and over the principle of authoritarianism, the ideal expression of that force which, after the destruction of all terrestrial and heavenly idols, will find and organize a new world of undivided mankind upon the ruins of all churches and States.

I am a convinced partisan of *economic and social equality,* for I know that outside this equality, freedom, justice, human dignity and moral and spiritual well-being of mankind and the prosperity of nations and individuals will always remain a lie only. But as an unconditional partisan of freedom, this first condition of humanity, I believe the equality must be established through the spontaneous organization of voluntary cooperation of work freely organized, and into communes federated, by productive associations and through the equally spontaneous federation of communes—*not through and by supreme and supervising action of the State.*

This point separates above all others the revolutionary socialists or collectivists from the authoritarian "communists", the adherents of the absolute initiative and necessity of and by the State. The communists imagine that condition of freedom and socialism (i.e., the administration of the society's affairs by the self-government of the society itself without the medium and pressure of the State) can be achieved by the development and organization of the political power of the working class, chiefly of the proletariat of the towns with the help of bourgeois radicalism, while the revolutionary (who are otherwise, known as libertarian) socialists, enemies of every double-edged allies and alliance believe, on the very contrary that the aim can be realised and materialized only through the development and organization not of the political but of the social and economic, and therefore anti-political forces of the working masses of the town and country, including all well disposed people of the upper classes who are ready to break away from their past and join them openly and accept their programme unconditionally.

Two Methods

From the difference named, there arise two different methods. The "Communists" pretend to organize the working classes in order to "capture the political power of the State". The revolutionary socialists organize people with the object of the liquidation of the States altogether whatever be their form. The first are the partisans of authoritiveness in theory and practice, the socialists have confidence only in freedom to develop the initiative of peoples in order to liberate themselves. The communist authoritarians wish to force class "science"

upon others, the social libertarians propagate emporicl science among them so that human groups and aggregation infused with conviction in and understanding of i spontaneously, freely and voluntarily, from bottom u₁ wards, organize themselves by their own motion and i the measure of their strength—not according to a pla sketched out in advance and dictated to them, a pla which is attempted to be imposed by a few "highly intelli gent, honest and all that" upon the so—called ig masses from above.

The revolutionary social libertarians think that the is much more practical reason and common sense in the aspirations and the real needs of the people than in th "deep" intelligence of all the learned men and tutors, mankind who want to add to the many disastro attempts "to make humanity happy" a still newe attempt. We are on the contrary of the conviction tha humankind has allowed itself too long enough to b governed and legislated for and that the origin of its misery is not to be looked for in this or that form o government and man-established State, but in the ver nature and existence of every ruling leadership, whatever kind and in whatever name this may be. Th best friends of the ignorant people are those who fre them from the thraldom of leadership and let peopl alone to work among themselves with one another o the basis of equal comradeship.

ESSAYS OF BAKUNIN

THE POLICY OF THE COUNCIL.
(1869)

I

The Council of Action does not ask any worker if he is of a religious or atheistic turn of mind. She does not ask if he belongs to this or that or no political party. She simply says: Are you a worker? If not, do you feel the necessity of devoting yourself wholly to the interests of the working class, and of avoiding all movements that are opposed to it? Do you feel at one with the workers? And have you the strength in you that is requisite if you would be loyal to their cause? Are you aware that the workers—who create all wealth, who have made civilisation and fought for liberty—are doomed to live in misery, ignorance, and slavery? Do you understand that the main root of all the evils that the workers experience, is poverty? And that poverty—which is the common lot of the workers in all parts of the world—is a consequence of the present economic organisation of society, and especially of the enslavement of labour—i. e. the proletariat—under the yoke of capitalism—i.e. the bourgeoisie.

Do you know that between the proletariat and the bourgeoisie there exists a deadly antagonism which is the logical consequence of the economic positions of the two classes? Do you know that the wealth of the bourgeoisie is incompatible with the comfort and liberty of the workers, because their excessive wealth is, and can only be, built upon the robbing and enslavement of the workers? Do you understand that, for the same reason, the prosperity and dignity of the labouring masses inevitably demands the entire abolition of the bourgeoisie Do you realise that no single worker, however intelligent and energetic he may be, can fight successfully against the excellently organised forces of the bourgeoisie—a force which is upheld mainly by the organisation of the State— all States?

Do you not see that, in order to become a power, you must unite—not with the bourgeoisie, which would be a folly and a crime, since all the bourgeoisie, so far as they belong to their class, are our deadly enemies?—Nor with such workers as have deserted their own cause and have lowered themselves to beg for the benevolence of the governing class ? But with the honest men, who are moving, in all sincerity, towards the same goal as you? Do you understand that, against the powerful combinations formed by the privileged classes, the capitalists or possessors of the means and instruments of production and distribution, **the divided or sectarian associations of labour, can ever triumph?** Do you not realise that, in order to fight and to vanquish this capitalist combination, nothing less than the amalgamation, in council and action, of all local, and national labour associations— federating into an international association of the workers of all lands,—is required.

If you know and comprehend all this, come into our camp whatever else your political or religious convictions are. But if you are at one with us, and so long as you are at one with us, you will wish to pledge the whole of your being, by your every action as well as by your words, to the common cause, as a spontaneous and whole-hearted expression of that fervour of loyalty that will inevitably take possession of you. You will have to promise:

(1) To subordinate your personal and even your family interest, as well as political and religious bias and would be activities, to the highest interest of our association, namely the struggle of labour against Capital, the economic fight of the Proletariat against the Bourgeoisie.

(2) Never, in your personal interests, to compromise with the bourgeoisie.

(3) Never to attempt to secure a position above your fellow workers, whereby you would become at once a bourgeois and an enemy of the proletariat: for the only difference between capitalists and workers is this: the former seek their welfare outside, and at the expense of, the welfare of the community whilst the welfare of the latter is dependent on the solidarity of those who are robbed on the industrial field.

(4) To remain ever and always to this principle of the solidarity of labour: for the smallest betrayal of this principle, the slightest deviation from this solidarity, is, in the eyes of the International, the greatest crime and shame with which a worker can soil himself.

II

The pioneers of the Councils of Action act wisely in refusing to make philosophic or political principles the basis of their association, and preferring to have the exclusively economic struggle of Labour against Capital as the sole foundation. They are convinced that the moment a worker realises the class struggle, the moment he—trusting to his right and the numerical strength of his class—enters the arena against capitalist robbery: that very moment, the force of circumstances and the evolution of the struggle, will oblige him to recognise all the political, socialistic, and philosophic principles of the class-struggle. These principles are nothing more or less than the real expression of the aims and objects of the working-class. The necessary and inevitable conclusion of these aims, their one underlying and supreme purpose, is the abolition—from the political as well as from the social viewpoint—of:—

(1) The class-divisions existent in society, especially of those divisions imposed on society by, and in, the economic interests of the bourgeoisie.

(2) All Territorial States, Political Fatherlands and Nations, and on the top of the historic ruins of this old world order, the establishment of the great international federation of all local and national productive groups.

From the philosophic point of view, the aims of the working class are nothing less than the realisation of the eternal ideals of humanity, the welfare of man, the reign of equality, justice, and liberty on earth, making unnecessary all belief in heaven and all hopes for a better hereafter.

The great mass of the workers, crushed by their daily toil, live in ignorance and misery. Whatever the political and religious prejudices in which they have been reared individually may be, this mass is unconsciously Socialistic: instinctively, and, through the pinch of hunger and their position, more earnestly and truly Socialistic than all the "scientific" and "bourgeois Socialists" put together. The mass are Socialists through all the circumstances of reasoning; and, in reality, the necessities of life have a greater influence over those of pure reasoning, because reasoning (or thought) is only the reflex of the continually developing life-force and not its basis.

The workers do not lack reality, the zeal for Socialist endeavour, but only the Socialist idea. Every worker, from the bottom of his heart, is longing for a really human existence, i.e. material comfort and mental development founded on justice, i.e,, equality and liberty for each and every man in work. This cannot be realised in the existing political and social organisation, which is founded on injustice and bare-faced robbery of the labouring masses. Consequently, every reflective worker becomes a revolutionery Socialist, since he is forced to realise that his emancipation can only be accomplished by the complete overthrow of present-day society. Either this organisation of injustice with its entire machine of oppressive laws and priviledged institutions, must disappear, or else the proletariat is condemned to eternal slavery.

This is the quintessence of the Socialist idea, whose germs can be found in the instinct of every serious thinking worker. Our object, therefore, is to make him conscious of what he wants, to awaken in him a clear idea that corresponds to his instincts: for the moment the class consciousness of the proletariat has lifted itself up to the level of their instinctive feeling, their intention will have developed into determination, and their power will be irresistible.

What prevents the quicker development of this idea of salvation amongst the Proletariat? Its ignorance; and, to a great extent, the political and religious prejudices with which the governing classes are trying to befog the consciousness and the natural intelligence of the people. How can you disperse this ignorance and destroy these strange prejudices? "The liberation of the Proletariat must be the work of the Proletariat itself," says the preface to the general statute of the (First) International. And it is a thousand times true! This is the main foundation of our great association. But the working class is still very ignorant. It lacks completely every theory. There is only one way out therefore, namely—<u>Proletarian liberation through action</u>. And what will this action be that will bring the masses to Socialism? It is the economic struggle of the Proletariat against the governing class carried out in solidarity. It is the Industrial Organisation of the workers—the Council of Action.

THE ORGANISATION OF THE INTERNATIONAL.

(1869)

The masses are the social power, or, at least, the essence of that power. But they lack two things in order to free themselves from the hateful conditions which oppress them: education and organisation. These two things represent, to-day, the real foundations of power of all government.

To abolish the military and governing power of the State, the proletarian must organise. But since organisation cannot exist without knowledge, it is necessary to spread among the masses real social education.

To spread this real social education is the aim of the International. Consequently, the day on which the International succeeds in uniting in its ranks a half, a fourth, or even a tenth part of the workers of Europe, the State or States will cease to exist. The organisation of the International will be altogether different from the organisation of the State, since its aim is not to create new States but to destroy all existing government systems. The more artificial, brutal, and authoritarian is the power of the State, the more indifferent and hostile it is to the natural developments, interests and desires of the people, the freer and more natural must be the organisation of the International. It must try all the more to accommodate itself to the natural instincts and ideals of the people.

But what do we mean by the natural organisation of the masses? We mean the organisation which is founded upon the experience and results of their everyday life and the difference of their occupations, *i.e.*, their industrial organisation. The moment all branches of industry are represented in their International, the organisation of the masses will be complete.

But it might be said that, since we exercise, through the International, organised influence over the masses, we are aiming at new power equally with the politicians of the old State systems. This change is a great mistake. The influences of the International over the masses differs from all government power in that, it is no more than a natural, unofficial influence of ordinary ideas, without authority.

The State is the authority, the rule, and organised power of the possessing class, and the make-believe experts over the life and liberty of masses. The State does not want anything other than the servility of the masses. Hence it demands their submission.

The International, on the other hand, has no other object than the absolute freedom of the masses. Consequently, it appeals to the rebel instinct. In order that this rebel instinct should be strong and powerful enough to overthrow the rule of the State and the privileged class, the International must organise.

To reach this goal, it has to employ two quite just weapons :

    (1) The propagation of its ideas.

    (2) The natural organisation of its power or authority, through the influence of its adherents on the masses.

A person who can assert that, such organised activity is an attack on the freedom of the masses, or an attempt to create a new rule, is either a sophist or a fool. It is sad enough for those who don't know the rules of human solidarity, to think that complete individual independence is possible, or desirable. Such a condition would mean the dissolution of all human society, since the entire social existence of man depends on the interdependence of individuals and the masses. Every person, even the cleverest and strongest—nay, especially the clever and strong—are at all times, the creatures as also the creators of this influence. The freedom of each individual is the direct outcome of those material mental and moral influences, of all individuals surrounding him in that society in which he lives, develops, and dies. A person who seeks to free himself from that influence in the name of a metaphysical, superhuman, and perfectly egotistical "freedom" aims at his own extermination as a human being. And those who refuse to use that influence on others, withdraw from all activity of social life, and by not passing on their thoughts and feelings, work for their own destruction. Therefore, this so-called "independence," which is preached so often by the idealists and metaphysicians: this so-called individual liberty is only the destruction of existence.

In nature, as well as in human society, which is never anything else than part of that same nature, every creature exists on condition that he tries, as much as his individuality will permit, to influence the lives of others. The destruction of that indirect [influence would mean death. And when we desire the freedom of the masses, we by no means want to destroy this natural influence, which individuals or groups of individuals, create through their own contract.

What we seek is the abolition of the artificial, privileged, lawful, and official influence. If the Church and State were private institutions, we should be, even then, I suppose their opponents. But we should not have protested against their right to exist. True, in a sense, they are, to-day, private institutions, as they exist exclusively to conserve the interests of the privileged classes. Still, we oppose them, because they use all the power of the masses to force their rule upon the latter in an authoritarian, official, and brutal manner. If the International could have organised itself in the State manner, we, its most enthusiastic friends, would have become its bitterest enemies. But it cannot possibly organise itself in such a form. The International cannot recognise limits to human fellowship and equality, whilst the State cannot exist unless it limits, by territorial pretensions, such fellowship and equality. History has shown us that the realisation of a league of all the States of the world, about which all the despots have dreamt, is impossible. Hence those who speak of the State, necessarily think and speak of a world divided into different States, who are internally oppressors and outwardly despoilers, *i.e.*, enemies to each other. The State, since it involves this division, oppression, and despoilation of humanity, must represent the negation of humanity and the destruction of human society.

There would not have been any sense in the organisation of the workers at all, if they had not aimed at the overthrow of the State. The International organises the masses with this object in view, to the end that they might reach this goal. And how does it organise them ?

Not from the top to the bottom, by imposing a seeming unity and order on human society, as the state attempts, without regards to the differences of interest arising from differences of occupation. On the contrary, the International organises the masses from the bottom upwards, taking the social life of the masses, their real aspirations as a starting point, and encouraging them to unite in groups according to their real interests in society. The International evolves a unity of purpose and creates a real equilibrium of aim and well-being out of their natural difference in life and occupation.

Just because the International is organised in this way, it develops a real power. Hence it is essential that every member of every group should be acquainted thoroughly with all its principles. Only by these means will he make a good propagandist in time of peace and real revolutionist in time of war.

We all know that our program is just. It expresses in a few noble words the just and humane demands of the proletariat. Just because it is an absolutely humane program, it contains all the symptoms of the social revolution. It proclaims the destruction of the old and the creation of the new world.

This is the main point which we must explain to all members of the International. This program substitutes a new science, a new philosophy for the old religion. And it defines a new international policy, in place of the old diplomacy. It has no other object than the overthrow of the States.

In order that the members of the International scientifically fill their posts, as revolutionary propagandists, it is necessary for every one to be imbued with the new science, philosophy, and policy: the new spirit of the International. It is not enough to declare that we want the economic freedom of the workers, a full return for our labour, the abolition of classes, the end of political slavery, the realisation of all human rights, equal duties and justice for all: in a phrase, the unity of humanity. All this, is, without a doubt, very good and just. But when the workers of the international simply go on repeating these phrases, without grasping their truth and meaning, they have to face the danger of reducing their just claims to empty words, cant which is mouthed without understanding.

It might be answered that not all workers, even when they are members of the International, can be educated. It is not enough, then, that there are in the organisation, a group of people, who—as far as possible—are acquainted with the science, philosophy, and policy of Socialism? Cannot the wide mass follow their " brotherly advice " not to turn from the right path, that leads ultimately to the freedom of the proletariat ?

The authoritarian Communists in the International often make use of these arguments, although they have wanted the courage to state them so freely and so clearly. They have sought to hide their real opinion under demagogic compliments about the cleverness and all powerfulness of the people. We were always the bitterest enemies of this opinion. And we are convinced, that, if the International split into two groups—a big majority, and small minority of ten, twenty or more people—in such a way, that the majority were convinced blindly of the theoretical and practical sense of the minority, the result would be the reduction of the International to an oligarchy—the worst form of State. The educated and capable minority would, together with its responsibilities, demand the rights of a governing body. And this governing body would prove more despotic than an avowed autocracy, because it would be hidden beneath a show of servile respect for the will of the people. The minority would rule through the medium of resolutions, imposed upon the people, and afterwards called " the will of the people." In this way, the educated minority would develop into a government, which, like all other governments, would grow every day more despotic and reactionary.

The International only then can become a weapon for

liberating the people, when it frees itself; when it does not permit itself to be divided into two groups—a big majority, the blind tool of an educated minority. That is why its first duty is to imprint upon the minds of its members the science, philosophy, and policy of Socialism.

THE WORKERS AND THE SPHINX.
(1867)

1. The Council of Action claims for each the full product of his labour : meaning by that his complete and equal right to enjoy, in common with his fellow-workers, the full amenities of life and happiness that the collective labour of the people creates. The Council declares that it is wrong for those who produce nothing at all to be able to maintain their insolent riches, since they do so only by the work of others. Like the Apostle Paul, the Council maintains, that, " if any would not work, neither should he eat."

The Council of Action avers that the right to the noble name of labour belongs exclusively to productive labor. Some years ago, the young King of Portugal paid a visit to his august father-in-law. He was presented to a gathering of the Working Men's Association at Turin : and there, surrounded by workers, he uttered these memorable words : "**Gentlemen, the present century is the century of labor. We all labor. I, too, labor for the good of my people.**"

However flattering this likening of royal labor to working-class labor may appear, we cannot accept it. We must recognise that royal labor is a labor of absorption and not of production. Capitalists, proprietors, contractors also labor : but all such labor is parasitic, since it has no other object than to transfer the real products of labour from the hands of the workers, whose toil creates them, into the possession of those who do not create them, to serve the purpose of further gain and exploitation. Such labor cannot be considered productive labor. In this sense, thieves and brigand labor also. Roughly, they risk every day their liberty and their life. But they do not work.

The Council of Action recognises intellectual labor—that of men of science—as productive labor. It places the application of science to industry, and the activity of the organisers and administrators of industrial and commercial affairs, in the category of useful or productive labor. But it demands for all men a participation as much in manual labor as in the labor of the mind. The question of how much manual and how much mental labor a person shall contribute to the community must be decided not by the privileges of birth of social status, but by suitability to the natural capacities of each, developed by equal opportunity of education and instruction.

Only thus can class distinctions and privileges disappear and the cant phrase, "the intelligent and working masses" be relegated to deserved oblivion.

2 The Council of Action declares that, so long as the working masses are plunged in the misery of economic servitude, all so-called reforms and even so-called political revolutions of a seeming proletarian character, will avail them nothing. They are condemned to live in a forced ignorance and to accept a slave status by the economic organisation of wage-slave society.

3. Consequently, the Council of Action urges the workers in their own interests, material as well as moral,—and moral because so completely and thoroughly and equally material for each and all—to subordinate **all seeming political questions to definite economic issues.** The material means of an education and of an existence really human, are for the proletariat, the first condition of liberty, morality and humanity.

4. The Council of Action declares that the record of past centuries, the class legacy of exploitation, as well as contemporary experience, should have convinced the workers that they can expect no social amelioration of their lot from the generosity of the privileged classes. There is no justice in class society, since justice can exist only in equality; and equality means the abolition of class and privilege. (Monopoly) There never has been and there never will be a generous or just ruling class. The classes and orders existing in present day-society—clergy, bureaucracy, plutocracy, nobility, bourgeoisie—dispute for power only to consolidate their own strength and to increase their profits within the system. **The Council of Action exists to express the truth that, henceforth, the proletariat must take the direction of its own affairs into its own hands.**

5. Once the proletariat clearly understands itself, its solidarity will find expression in the Council of action, or Federated Councils of Action. Then there will remain no power in the world that can resist the workers.

6. To this end, the Council of Action affirms that the proletariat ought to tend, not to the establishment of a new rule or of a new class for its alleged profit as a class, but

to the definite abolition of all rule, of every class. Dictatorship, political sectarianism, all spell power, exploitation, and injustice. The proletariat, through their Council of Action organisation, must express the organisation of justice liberty, without distinction of race, color, nationality, or faith—all to fully exercise the same duties and enjoy the same rights.

7. The cause of the working class of the entire world is one, is solidarity, across and in spite of all State frontiers. Expressing that common purpose, that complete proletarian identity of interest, the Council of Action proclaims the International one-ness of the workers' cause. It pioneers the definite International Association of the Workers of the World in a chain of Industrial Associations. The cause of the workers is International because, pushed by an inevitable law which is inherent in it, bourgeois capital in its threefold employment—in industry, commerce and in banking speculations—has been tending, since the beginning of the nineteenth century, towards an organisation more and more International and complete, enlarging each day more, and simultaneous in all countries, the abyss which separates the working world from the bourgeois world. From this fact, it results that, for every worker endowed with intelligence and heart, for every proletaire who has vision and affection for his companions in misery and servitude; who is conscious of the situation of himself and his class and of his actual interest: the real country is henceforth the International Camp of Labor. And the true local organisation of that camp is the Council of Action.

To every worker, truly worthy of the name, the workers of so-called foreign countries, who suffer and are oppressed as he is oppressed, are infinitely nearer and of more immediate kin than the bourgeoisie of his own country, who enrich themselves to his detriment. Because of this the Council of Action will replace the geographical unit of false democracy, the National State.

8. The deliverance of the proletariat from the oppression and exploitation which it endures in all countries alike, must be International. In those lands which are bound by means of credit, industry, and commerce, the economic and social emancipation of the proletariat must be achieved almost simultaneously by a common struggle ending in a triumphant challenge to the existing political constitution of the world. The economic emancipation of the proletariat is the foundation of the political emancipation of the world. Realising this, the Council of Action preaches the proletarian duty and message of fraternity.

By the duty of fraternity, as well as by the call of enlightened self-interest, the workers are called upon to establish, organise, and exercise the greatest practical solidarity, industrial, communal, provincial, national and international: beginning in their workshop, their home, their tenement, their street, their political group and extending it to all their trade societies, to all their trade propaganda federations, a close industrial solidarity. They ought to observe this solidarity scrupulously, and practice it in all the developments, catastrophes, and incidents of the incessant daily struggle of the labor of the worker against the stolen capital of the bourgeois; all those demands and claims of hours and wages, strikes, and every question that relates to the existence, whether material or moral, of the working people.

The revolt of the workers and the spontaneous organisation of human solidarity through the free but involuntary and inevitable federation of all working-class groups into the Council of Action ! This, then, is the answer to the enigma which the Capitalist Sphinx forces us to-day to solve, threatening to devour us if we do not solve it.

SOLIDARITY IN LIBERTY

The Workers Path To Freedom
(1867)

From this truth of practical solidarity or fraternity of struggle that I have laid down as the first principle of the Council of Action flows a theoretical consequence of equal importance. The workers are able to unite as a class for class economic action, because all religious philosophies, and systems of morality which prevail in any given order of society are always the ideal expression of its real, material situation. Theologies, philosophies and ethics define, first of all, the economic organisation of society; and secondly, the political organisation, which is itself nothing but the legal and violent consecration of the economic order. Consequently, there are not several religions of the ruling class; there is one, the religion of property. And there are not several religions of the working class: there is one, the piety of struggle, the vision of emancipation, penetrating the fog of every mysticism, and finding utterance in a thousand prayers. Workers of all creeds, like workers of all lands, have but one faith, hope, and charity; one common purpose overleaps the barriers of seeming hatreds of race and creed. The workers are one class, and therefore one race, one faith, one nation. This is the theoretical truth to be induced from the practical fraternal solidarity of the Council of Action organisation. Church and State are liquidated in the vital organisation of the working class, the genius of free humanity.

It has been stated that Protestantism established liberty in Europe. This is a great error. It is the economic, material emancipation of the bourgeois class which, in spite of Protestantism, has created that exclusively political and legal liberty, which is too easily confounded with the grand, universal, human liberty, which only the proletariat can create. The necessary accompaniment of bourgeois legal and political liberty, appearances to the contrary notwithstanding, is the intellectual, anti-Christian, and anti-religious emancipation of the bourgeoisie. The capitalist ruling class has no religion, no ideals, and no illusion. It is cynical and unbelieving because it denies the real base of human society, the complete emancipation of the working class. Bourgeois society, by its very nature of interested professionalism, must maintain centres of authority and exploitation, called States. The labourers, by their very economic needs, must challenge such centres of oppression.

The inherent principles of human existence are summed up in the single law of solidarity. This is the golden rule of humanity, and may be formulated thus: no person can recognise or realise his or her own humanity except by recognising it in others and so co-operating for its realisation by each and all. No man can emancipate himself save by emancipating with him all the men about him.

My liberty is the liberty of everybody. I cannot be free in idea until I am free in fact. To be free in idea and not free in fact is to be revolt. To be free in fact is to have my liberty and my right, find their confirmation, and sanction in the liberty and right of all mankind. I am free only when all men are my equals. (first and foremost economically.)

What all other men are is of the greatest importance to me. However independent I may imagine myself to be, however far removed I may appear from mundane considerations by my social status, I am enslaved to the misery of the meanest member of society. The outcast is my daily menace. Whether I am Pope, Czar, Emperor, or even Prime Minister, I am always the creature of their circumstance, the conscious product of their ignorance, want and clamouring. They are in slavery, and I, the superior one, am enslaved in consequence.

For example if such is the case, I am enlightened or intelligent man. But I am foolish with the folly of the people, my wisdom stunned by their needs, my mind palsied. I am a brave man, but I am the coward of the peoples' fear. Their misery appals me, and every day I shrink from the struggle of life. My career becomes an evasion of living. A rich man, I tremble before their poverty, because it threatens to engulf me. I discover I have no riches in myself, no wealth but that stolen from the common life of the common people. As privileged man, I turn pale before the people's demand for justice. I feel a menace in that demand. The cry is ominous and I am threatened. It is the feeling of the malefactor dreading, yet waiting for inevitable arrest. My life is privileged and furtive. But it is not mine. I lack freedom and contentment. In short, wishing to be free, though I am wise, brave, rich, and privileged, I cannot be free because my immediate associates do not wish men to be free; and the mass, from whom all wisdom, bravery, riches, and privileges ascend, do not know how to secure their freedom. The slavery of the common people make them the instruments of my oppression. For me to be free, they must be free. We must conquer bread and freedom in common.

The true, human liberty of a single individual implies the emancipation of all: because, thanks to the law of solidarity, which is the natural basis of all human society, I cannot be, feel, and know myself really, completely free, if I am not surrounded by men as free as myself. The slavery of each is my slavery.

It follows that the question of individual liberty is not a personal but a social economic question that depends on the deliverance of the proletariat for its realisation. That in turn, involves the spontaneous organisation and capacity for economic and social action through the voluntary and free grouping of all workers' organisations into the Council of Action. The Red Association of those who toil!

THE RED ASSOCIATION
(1870)

Political freedom without economic equality is a pretence, a fraud, a lie; and the workers want no lying.

The workers necessarily strive after a fundamental transformation of society, the result of which must be the abolition of classes, equally in economic as in political respects: after a system of society in which all men will enter the world under special conditions, will be able to unfold and develop themselves, work and enjoy the **good** things of life. These are the demands of justice.

But how can we from the abyss of ignorance, of misery and slavery, in which the workers on the land and in the cities are sunk, arrive at that paradise, the realisation of justice and manhood? For this the workers have one means: the Association of Councils.

Through the Association they brace themselves up, they mutually improve each other and, through their own efforts, make an end of that dangerous ignorance which is the main support of their slavery. By means of the Association, they learn to help, and mutually support one another. Thereby they will reach, finally, a power which will prove more powerful than all confederated bourgeois capital and political powers put together.

The Council must become *the* Association in the mind of every worker. It must become the password of every political and agitational organisation of the workers, the password of every group, in every industry throughout all lands. Undoubtedly the Council is the weightiest and most hopeful sign of the proletarian struggle an infallible omen of the coming complete emanicipation of the workers.

Experience has proved that the isolated associations are not more powerful than are the isolated workers. Even the Association of all Workers' Associations of a single country would not be sufficiently powerful to stand up in conflict with the international combination of all profit-making world capital. Economic science establishes the fact that the emancipation of the worker is no national question. No country, no matter how wealthy, mighty, and well-served it may be, can undertake—without ruining itself and surrendering its inhabitants to misery—a fundamental alteration in the relations twixt capital and labor, if this alteration is not accomplished, at the same time, at least, in the greatest part of the industrial countries of the world. Consequently, the question of the emancipation of the worker from the yoke of capital and its representatives, the bourgeois capitalists, is, above all, an international question. Its solution, therefore, is only possible through an International Movement.

Is this International Movement a secret idea, a conspiracy? Not in the least. The International Movement, the Council Association, does not dictate from above or prescribe in secret. It federates from below and wills from a thousand quarters. It speaks in every group of workers and embraces the combined decision of all factions. The Council is living democracy; and whenever the Association formulates plans, it does it openly, and speaks to all who will listen. Its word is the voice of labour recruiting its energies for the overthrow of capitalist oppression.

What does the Council say? What is the demand it makes through every association of those who toil and think, in every factory, in every country? What does it request?

Justice! The strictest justice and the rights of humanity: the right of manhood, womanhood, childhood, irrespective of all distinctions of birth, race, or creed. The right to live and the obligation to work to maintain that right. Service from each to all and from all to each. If this idea appears appalling and prodigious to the existent bourgeois society, so much the worse for this society.

Is the Council of Action a revolutionary enterprise? Yes and no.

The Council of Action is revolutionary in the sense that it will replace a society based upon injustice, exploitation, privilege, laziness, and authority, by one which is founded upon justice and freedom for all mankind. In a word, it wills an economic, political, and social organisation, in which each person, without prejudice to his natural and personal idiosyncrasies, will find it equally possible to develop himself, to learn, to think, to work, to be active, and to enjoy life honourably. Yes, this it desires; and we repeat, once more, if this is incompatible with the existing organisation of society, so much the worse for this society.

Is the Council of Action revolutionary in the sense of barricades and of violent uprising or demonstration? No; the Council concerns itself but little with this kind of politics; or, rather, one should say that the Council takes no part in it whatever. The bourgeois revolutionaries, anxious for some change of power, and police agents finding occupation in passing explosions of sound and fury, are annoyed greatly with the Council of Action on account of the Council's indifference towards their activities and schemes of provocation.

The Council of Action, the Red Association of those who want and toil, comprehended, long since, that each bourgeois politic—no matter how red and revolutionary it might appear—served not the emancipation of the workers, but the tightening of their slavery. Even if the Council had not comprehended this fact, the miserable game, which, at times, the bourgeois republican and even the bourgeois Socialist plays, would have opened the workers' eyes.

The Council of Action, ever evolving more completely into the International Workers' Movement, holds itself severely aloof from the dismal political intrigues, and knows to-day only one policy: to each group and to each worker: his propaganda, its extension and organisation into struggle and action. On the day when the great proportion of the world's workers have associated themselves through Council of Actions, and so firmly organised through Council of Actions, and so firmly organised through their divisions into one common solidarity of movement, no revolution, in the sense of violent insurrection, will be necessary. From this it will be seen that anarchists do not stand for abortive violence which its enemies attribute to it. Without violence, justice will triumph. Oppression will be liquidated by the direct power of the workers through association. And if that day, there are impatient heads, and some suffering, this will be the guilt of the bourgeoisie refusing to recognise what has happend, through their machination. To the triumph of the social revolution itself, violence will be unnecessary.

THE CLASS WAR
(1870)

Except Proudhon and M. Louis Blanc almost all the historians of the revolution of 1848 and of the coup d'etat of December, 1851, as well as the greatest writers of bourgeois radicalism, the Victor Hugos, the Quinets, etc. have commented at great length on the crime and the criminals of December; but they have never deigned to touch upon the crime and the criminals of June. And yet it is so evident that December was nothing but the fatal consequence of June and its repetition on a large scale.

Why this silence about June? Is it because the criminals of June are bourgeois republicans of whom the above named writers have been, morally, more or less accomplices? Accomplices in their principles and therefore indirectly accomplices to their acts. This reason is probable, but there is yet another which is certain. The crime of June struck workers only, revolutionary socialists, consequently strangers to the class and natural enemies of the principles that all these honourable writers represent. The crime of December attacked and deported thousands of bourgeois republicans, the social brothers of these honourable writers and their political co-religionists. Besides, they themselves have been its victims. Hence their extreme sensibilities to the December crimes, and their indifference to those of June.

A general rule: A bourgeois, however red a republican he be, will be much more keenly affected, aroused and smitten by a mishap to another bourgeois were this bourgeois even a mad imperialist than by the misfortune of a worker, of a man of the people. There is undoubtedly a great injustice in this difference, but the injustice is not premeditated. It is instinctive. It arises out of the conditions and habits of life which exercise a much greater influence over men than their ideas and political convictions. Conditions and habits, their special manner of existing, developing, thinking and acting; all their social relationships so manifold and various, and yet so regularly convergent towards the same aim; all this diversity of interest expressing common social ambition and constituting the life of the bourgeois world, establishes between those who belong to this world a solidarity infinitely more real, deeper, and unquestionably more sincere than any that might arise between a section of the bourgeoisie and the workers. No difference of political opinions is sufficient to overcome the bourgeois community of interests. No seeming agreement of political opinions is sufficient to overcome the antagonism of interests that divide the bourgeoisie from the workers. Community of convictions and ideas are and must ever be subsidiary to a community of class interests and prejudices.

Life dominates thought and determines the will. This is a truth that should never be lost sight of when we wish to understand anything about social and political phenomena. If we wish to establish a sincere and complete community of thought and will between men, we must found it on similar conditions of life, or on a community of interests. And as there is, by the very conditions of their respective existence, an abyss between the bourgeois world and the world of the worker,—the one being the exploiting world, the other the world of the victimised and exploited,—I conclude that if a man born and brought up in the bourgeois environment wishes to become sincerely and unreservedly the friend and brother of the workers, he must renounce all the conditions of his past existence; and outgrow all his bourgeois habits. He must break off his relations of sentiment with the bourgeois world, its vanity and ambition. He must turn his back upon it and become its enemy; proclaim irreconcilable war; and throw himself wholeheartedly into the world and cause of the worker.

If his passion for justice is too weak to inspire him to such resolution and audacity, let him not deceive himself and let him not deceive the workers. He can never become their friend and at every crisis must prove their enemy. His abstract thoughts, his dreams of justice will easily influence him in hours of calm reflection when nothing stirs in the exploited world. But let the moment of struggle come when the armed truce gives place to the irreconcilable conflict, his interests will compel him to serve in the camp of the exploiters. This has happened to our one-time friends in the past. It will happen again to many good republicans and socialists who have not lost their attachment to the bourgeois world.

Social hatreds are like religious hatreds. They are intense and deep. They are not shallow like political hatred. This fact explains the indulgence shown by the bourgeois democrats for the Bonapartists. It explains also their excessive severity against the socialist revolutionaries. They detest the former much less than the latter because of the pressure of economic interests. Consequently they unite with the Bonapartists to form a common reaction against the oppressed masses.

THE GERMAN CRISIS.
(1870)

Whosoever mentions the State, implies force, oppression, exploitation, injustice—all these brought together as a system are the main condition of present-day society. The State has never had, and never can have, a morality. Its only morality and justice is its own interest, its existence, and its omnipotence at any price; and before its interest, all interest of Humanity must stand in the background. The State is the negation of Humanity. It is this in two ways: the opposite of human freedom and human justice (internally), as well as the forcible disruption of the common solidarity of mankind (externally).

The Universal State, repeatedly attempted, has always proved an impossibility, so that, as long as *the State* exists, *States* will exist; and since every State regards itself as absolute, and proclaims the adoration of its power as the highest law, to which all other laws must be subordinated, it therefore follows that as long as State exist wars cannot cease. Every State must conquer, or be conquered. Every State must build its power on the weakness or, if it can do it without danger to itself, on the destruction, of other States.

To strive for international justice, liberty, and perpetual peace, and at the same time to uphold the State, is contradictory and naive. It is impossible to alter the nature of the State, because it is just this nature that constitutes the State; and States cannot change their nature without ceasing to exist. It thus follows that there cannot be a good, just, virtuous State. All States are bad in that sense, that they, by their nature, by their principle, by their very foundation and the highest ideal, of their existence, are the opponents of human liberty, morality, and justice. And in this regard there is, one may say what one likes, no great difference between the barbaric Russian Empire and the civilised States of Europe. Wherein lies the only difference ? Russian Tsardom does openly what the others do under the mask of hypocrisy. Tsardom, with its undisguised political method, and its contempt for humanity, is the only goal to which all statesmen of Europe secretly but envyingly aspire. All States of Europe do the same as Russia, as far as public opinion, and especially as far as the reawakened but very powerful solidarity of the people allow them—a public opinion and solidarity which contain in themselves the germs of the destruction of States. There is no "good"

State, with the possible exception of those that are powerless. And even they are quite criminal enough in their dreams.

He who wants freedom, justice, and peace, he who wants the entire (economic and political) liberation of the masses, must strive for the destruction of the States, and the establishment of a universal federation of free groups for Production.

As long as the German workers strive for the establishment of a national State—however popular and free they may imagine this State (and there is a far step from imagination to realisation, especially when there is the fraternisation of two diametrically opposed principles, the State and the liberty of the people, involved)—so long will they sacrifice the liberty of the people to the might of the State, Socialism to politics, international justice and fraternity to patriotism. It is clear that their own economic liberation will remain a beautiful dream, looming in the distant future.

It is impossible to reach two opposite poles simultaneously. Socialism, the Social Revolution, presupposes the abolition of the State; it is therefore clear that he who is in favour of the State must give up Socialism, and sacrifice the economic liberation of the workers to the political power of some privileged party.

The German Social-Democratic Party is forced to sacrifice the economic liberation of the proletariat, and consequently also their political liberation—or, better expressed, their liberation from politics—to the self-seeking and triumph of the bourgeois Democracy. This follows unquestionably from Articles 2 and 3 of their programme.* The first three paragraphs of Article 2 are quite in accord with the Socialist principles of the International, whose programme they copy nearly literally. But the fourth paragraph of the same article, which declares that political liberty is the forerunner of economic liberty, entirely destroys the practical value of the recognition of our principles. It can mean nothing else than this:—

"Proletarians, you are slaves, the victims of private property and capitalism. You want to liberate yourselves from this yoke. This is good, and your demands are quite just. But in order to realise them, you must help us to accomplish the political revolution. Afterwards we will help you to accomplish the Social Revolution. Let us, therefore, through the might of your arms establish the Democratic State, and then——and then we will create a commonweal for you, similar to the one the Swiss workers enjoy."

In order to convince oneself that this preposterous delusion expresses entirely the spirit and tendency of the German Social Democratic Party—*i. e.*, their programme, not the natural aspirations of the German workers, of whom the party consists—one need only study the third article of this programme, wherein all the initial demands, which shall be brought about by the peaceful and legal agitation of the party, are elaborated. All these demands, with the exception of the tenth, which had not even been proposed by the authors of the programme, but had been added later—during the discussion, by a member of the Eisenach Congress—all these demands are of an entirely political character. All those points which are recommended as the main object of the immediate practical activity of the party consist of nothing else but the well-known programme of bourgeois Democracy; universal suffrage, with direct legislation by the people, abolition of all political privilege; a citizen army; separation of Church and State, and school and State; free and compulsory education; liberty of the Press, assembly, and combination; conversion of all indirect taxation into a direct, progressive, and universal income-tax.

These are the true objects, the real goal of the party! An exclusively political reform of the State, the institutions and laws of the State. Am I not, therefore, entitled to assert that this programme is in reality a purely political and bourgeois affair, which looks upon Socialism only as a dream for a far distant future? Have I not likewise a right to assert that if one would judge the Social Democratic Party of the German workers by their programme— of which I will beware, because I know that the real aspirations of the German working class go infinitely further than this programme—then one would have a right to believe that the creation of this party had no other purpose than the exploitation of the mass of the proletariat as blind and sacrificed tools towards the realisation of the political plans of the German bourgeois Democracy.

ON THE SOCIAL UPHEAVAL.

Le Reveil du Peuple for September and October, 1870, published an important summary of an article by Michael Bakunin on the question of the social upheaval. Bakunin denounces all forms of reformist activity as being inimical to the emancipation of the working class, and proceeds to attack those who advocate a mere political revolution, brought about according to the constitutional forms of capitalist society, and through the medium of its parliamentary machine, in opposition to a direct social revolutionary change effected by the workers through the medium of their own political industrial organisation.

Bakunin argues that the fact that wages practically never rise above the bare level of subsistence renders it impossible for the workers to secure increased wellbeing under bourgeois society. With the progress of capitalist civilisation, the gulf between the two classes gapes wider and wider.

"It follows from this also, that in the most democratic and free countries, such as England, Belgium, Switzerland, and the U. S. A., the freedom and politcal rights which the workers enjoy ostensibly are merely fictitious. They, who are slaves to their masters in the social sense are slaves also in the political sense. They have neither the education, nor the leisure, nor the independence which are so absolutely necessary for the free and thoughtful exercise of their rights of citizenship. In the most democratic countries, those in which there is universal suffrage, they have one day of mastery, or rather of Saturnalia, Election day. Once this day, the bourgeoisie, their daily oppressors and exploiters, come before them, hat in hand and talk of equality, brotherhood, and call them a sovereign people, whose very humble servants and representatives they wish to be. Once this day is passed, fraternity and equality disperse like smoke; the bourgeoisie become once more the bourgeoisie; and the proletariat, the sovereign people, continue in their slavery. This is why the system of representative democracy is so much applauded by the radical bourgeoisie," even when in a popular direction, it is improved, completed, and developed through the referendum and the direct legislation of the people, in which form it is so strenuously advocated by a certain school of Germans, who strongly call themselves Socialists.

For, so long as the people remain slaves economically, they will also remain slaves politically, express their sentiments as such, and subordinate themselves to the bourgeoisie, who rely upon the continuance of the vote system for the preservation of their authority.

Does that mean that we revolutionary Socialists are opposed to universal suffrage, and prefer limited suffrage or the despotism of an individual ? By no means. What we assert is, that, universal suffrage *in itself*, **based as it is on economic and** social inequality, will never be for the people anything but a bait, and that from the side of democratic bourgeoisedom, it will never be aught but a shameful lie, the surest implement for strengthening, with a makebelieve of liberalism and justice, the eternal domination of the exploiting and owing classes, and so suppressing the freedom and interests of the people.

"Consequently we deny that the universal franchise in itself is a means in the hands of the people for the achievement of economic and social equality.

"On this ground we assert that the so-called Social Democrats, who, in those countries, where universal suffrage does not exist yet, exert themselves to persuade the people that they must achieve this before all else—as to-day the leaders of the Social Democratic Party are doing when they tell the people that political freedom is a necessary condition to the attainment of economic freedom—are themselves either the victims of a fatal error or they are charlatans. Do they really not know, or do they pretend not to know, that this preceding political freedom, *i.e.*, that which necessarily exists without economic and social equality, since it should have to precede these two fundamental equalities, will be essentially bourgeois freedom, *i.e.*, founded on the economic dependence of the people, and consequently incapable of brining forth its opposite, the economic and social, and creating such economic freedom as leads to the exclusive freedom of only the bourgeoisie?

"Are these peculiar Social Democrats victims to a fallacy or are they betrayers? That is a very delicate question, which I prefer not to examine too closely. To me it is certain, that there are no worse enemies of the people than those who try to turn them away from the social upheaval, the only change that can give them real freedom, justice, and well being in order to draw them again into the treacherous path of reforms, or of revolutions of an exclusively political character whose tool, victim and deputy the social democracy always has been."

Bakunin then proceeds to point out that the social upheaval does not exclude the political one. It only means that the political institutions shall alter neither before nor after, but together with the economic institutions.

"The political upheaval, simultaneously with and really inseparable from the social upheaval, whose negative expression or negative manifestation it will, so to speak, be, will no longer be a reformation, but a grandoise **liquidation**.

"The people are instinctively mistrustful of every government. when you promise them nice things, they say:—'You talk so because you are not yet at the rudder.' A letter from John Bright to his electors, when he became minister, says:—'The voters should not expect him to act according to what he used to say: it is somewhat different speaking in opposition and different acting as a minister.' Similarly spoke a member of the international, a very honest Socialist, when in September, 1870, he became the perfect of a very republican minded department. He 'retains his old views, but now he is compelled to act in opposition to them."

Bakunin asserts that both are quite right. Therefore it does not avail to change the personnel of the government. He proceeds to treat of the inevitable corruption that follows from authority, and insists that everyone who attains to power must succumb to such corruption since he must serve and conserve ruling-class economic rights.

GOD OR LABOUR.

The two Camps.

You taunt us with disbelieving in God. We charge you with believing in him. We do not condemn you for this. We do not even indict you. We pity you. For the time of illusions is past. We cannot be deceived any longer.

Whom do we find under God's banner? Emperors, kings, the official and the officious world; our lords and our nobles; all the privileged persons of Europe whose names are recorded in the *Almana de Gotha*; all the guinea pigs of the industrial, commercial and banking world; the patented professors of our universities; the civil service servants; the low and high police officers; the gendarmes; the gaolers; the headsmen or hangmen, not forgetting the priests, who are now the black police enslaving our souls to the State; the glorious generals, defenders of the public order; and lastly, the writers of the reptile Press.

This is God's army!

Whom do we find in the camp opposite? The army of revolt; the audacious deniers of God and repudiators of all divine and authoritarian principles! Those who are therefore, the believers in humanity, the asserters of human liberty.

You reproach us with being Atheists. We do not complain of this. We have no apology to offer. We admit we are. With what pride is allowed to frail individuals—who, like passing waves, rise only to disappear again in the universal ocean of the collective life—we pride ourselves on being Atheists. Atheism is Truth—or, rather the real basis of all Truths.

We do not stoop to consider practical consequences. We want Truth above everything. *Truth for all!*

We believe in spite of all the apparent contradictions inspite of the wavering political wisdom of the Parliamentarians—and of the scepticism of the times—that truth only can make for the practical happiness of the people. This is our first article of faith.

It appears as if you were not satisfied in recording our Atheism. You jump to the conclusion that we can have neither love nor respect for mankind, inferring that all those great ideas or emotions which, in all ages, have set hearts throbbing are dead letters to us. Trailing at hazard our miserable existences—crawling, rather than walking, as you wish to imagine us—you asume that we cannot know of other feelings than the satisfaction of our coarse and sensual desires.

Do you want to know to what an extent we love the beautiful things that you revere? Know then that we love them so much that we are both angry and tired at seeing them hanging, out of reach, from your idealistic sky. We feel sorrow to see them stolen from our mother earth, transmuted into symbols without life, or into distant promises never to be realised. No longer are we satisfied with the fiction of things. We want them in their full reality. This is our second article of faith.

By hurling at us the epithet of materialists, you believe you have driven us to the wall. But you are greatly mistaken. Do you know the origin of your error?

What you and we call *matter* are two things totally different. Your *matter* is a fiction. In this it resembles your God, your Satan, and your immortal soul. Your matter is nothing beyond coarse lowness, brutal lifelessness. It is an impossible entity, as impossible as your pure spirit—"*immaterial*," "*absolute*"?

The first thinkers of makind were necessarily theologians and metaphysicians. Our earthly mind is so constituted that it begins to rise slowly—through a maze of ignorance—by errors and mistakes—to the possession of a minute parcel of Truth. This fact does not recommend "the glorious conditions of the past." But our theologians and metaphysicians, owing to their ignorance, took all that to them appeared to constitute power, movement, life, intelligence; and, by a sweeping generalisation, called it, *spirit*! To the lifeless and shapeless residue they thought remained after such preliminary selection—unconsciously evolved from the whole world of reality—they gave the name of *matter*! They were then surprised to see that this *matter*—which, like their *spirit* existed only in their imagination—appeared to be so lifeless and stupid when compared to their god, the eternal *spirit*! To be candid, we do not know *this God*. We do not recognise *this matter*.

By the words *matter* and *material*, we understand the totality of things, the whole gradation of phenomenal reality as we know it, from the most simple inorganic bodies to the complex functions of the mind of a man of genius; the most beautiful sentiments, the highest thoughts; the most heroic deeds; the actions of sacrifice and devotion; the duties and the rights, the abnegation and the egoism of our social life. The manifestations of organic life, the properties and qualities of simple bodies; electricity, light, heat, and molecular attraction, are all to our mind but so many different evolutions of that totality of things that we call *matter*. These evolutions are characterised by a close solidarity, a unity of motive power.

We do not look upon this totality of being and of forms as an eternal and absolute substance, as Panthetist do. But we look upon it as the *result*, always changed and always changing, of a variety of actions and reactions, and of the continuous working of real beings that are born and live in its very midst. Against the creed of the theologians I set these propositions:—

1. That if there were a God who created it the world could never have existed.

2. That if God were, or ever had been, the ruler of nature, natural, physical, and social law could never have existed. It would have presented a spectacle of complete chaos. Ruled from above, downwards, it would have resembled the calculated and designed disorder of the political State.

3. That moral law is a moral, logical and real law, only in so far as it emanates from the needs of human society.

4. That the idea of God is not necessary to the existence and working of the moral law. Far from this, it is a disturbing and socially demoralising factor.

5. That all gods, past and present, have owed their existence to a human imagination unfreed from the fetters of its primordial animality.

6. That any and every god, once established on his throne becomes the curse of humanity, and the natural ally of all tyrants, social charlatans, and exploiters of humanity.

7. That the routing of God will be a necessary consequence of the triumph of mankind. The abolition of the idea of God will be a fateful result of the proletarian emancipation.

From the moral point of view, Socialism is the advent of self respect to mankind. It will mean the passing of degradation and Divinity.

From the practical viewpoint, Socialism is the final acceptance of a great principle that is leavening society more and more every day. It is making itself more and more by the public conscience. It has bacome the basis of scientific investigations and progress, and of the proletariat. It is making its way everywhere. Briefly, this principle is as follows:

As in what we call the material world, the inorganic matter—mechanical, physical, and chemical—is the determinant basis of the organic matter—vegetable, animal intellectual—in like manner in the social world, the development of economical questions has been, and is the basis that determines our religious, philosophical, political, and social developments. On this subject Bakunin agrees with Marx.

This principle audaciously destroys all religious ideas and metaphysical beliefs. It is a rebellion far greater than that which, born during the Reniassance and the seventeenth century, levelled down all scholastic doctrine—once the powerful rampart of the Church, of the absolute monarchy, and of the feudal nobility—and brought about the dogmatic culture of the socalled pure reason, so favourable to our latter-day rulers the bourgeois classes. We therefore, say, through the International : The economical enslavement of the workers—to those who control the necessities of life and the instruments of labour, tools and machinery—is the sole and original cause of the present slavery in all its forms. To it are attributable mental degeneration and political submission. The economic emancipation of the workers, therefore, is the aim to which any political movement must subordinate its being, merely as a means to that end. This briefly is the central idea of the International.

POLITICS AND THE STATE
(1871)

We have repelled energetically every alliance with bourgeois politics, even of the most radical nature. It has been pretended, foolishly and slanderously, that we repudiated all such Political connivance because we were indifferent to the great question of Liberty, and considered only the economic or material side of the problem. It has been declared that, consequently, we placed ourselves in the ranks of the reaction. A German delegate at the Congress of Basle gave classic expression to this view, when he dared to state that, who ever did not recognise, with the German Socialists Democracy, "that the conquest of political rights (power) was the preliminary condition of social emancipation," was, consciously or unconsciously an ally, of the Ceasars !

These critics greatly deceive themselves and, "consciously or unconsciously," endeavour to deceive the public concerning us. We love liberty much more than they do. We love it to the point of wishing it complete and entire. We wish the reality and not the fiction. Hence we repel every bourgeois alliance, since we are convinced that all liberty conquered by the aid of the bourgeoisie, their political means and weapons, or by an alliance with their political dupes, will prove profitable for Messrs. the bourgeois, but never anything more than a fiction for the workers.

Messrs. the bourgeois of all parties, including the most advanced, however cosmopolitan they are, when it is a question of gaining money by a more and more extensive exploitation of the labour of the people, are all equally fervent and fanatical in their patriotic attachment to the state. Patriotism is in reality, nothing but the passion for and cult of the national State, as M. Thiers, the very illustrious assassin of the Parisian proletariat, and the present saviour of France, has said recently. But whoever says "State" says domination; and whoever says "domination" says exploitation. Which proves that the popular or "folk's" State, now become and unhappily remaining today the catchword of the German Socialist Democracy, is a ridiculous contradiction, a fiction, a falsehood, unconscious on the part of those who extol it, doubtlessly, but, for the proletariat, a very dangerous trap.

The State, however popular may be the form it assumes, will always be an institution of domination and exploitation, and consequently a permanent source of poverty and enslavement for the populace. There is no other way, then, of enancipating the people economically and politically, of giving them liberty and well-being at one and the same time, than by abolishing the State, all States, and, by so doing, killing, once and for all time, what, up to now, has been called "Politics," i. e., *precisely nothing else than the functioning or manifestation both internal and external of State action, that is to say, the practice, or art and science of dominating and exploiting the masses in favour of the privileged classes.*

It is not true then to say that we treat politics abstractly. We make no abstraction of it, since we wish positively to kill it. And here is the essential point upon which we separate ourselves absolutely from politicians and radical bourgeois Socialists (now functioning as social or radical democracy which is only a facade for capitalistic democracy,). Their policy consists in the transformation of State politics, their use and reform. Our policy, the only policy we admit, consists in the total abolition of the State, and of politics, which is its necessary manifestation.

It is only because we wish frankly to this abolition of the State that we believe that we have the right to call ourselves Internationalists and Revolutionary Socialists; for whoever wishes to deal with politics otherwise than how we do; whoever does not, like us, wish the total abolition of politics, must necessarily participate in the politics of a patriotic and bourgeois State. In other words, he renounces, by that very fact, in the name of his great or little national State, the human solidarity of all peoples, as well as the economic and social emancipation of the masses at home.

THE COMMUNE, THE CHURCH & THE STATE.

I am a passionate seeker for truth and just as strong an opponent of the corrupting lies, through which the party of order—this privileged, official, and interested representative of all religions, philosophical, political, legal economical, and social outrage in the past and present— has tried to keep the world in ignorance. I love freedom with all my heart. It is the only condition under which the intelligence, the manliness, and happiness of the people, can develop and expand. By freedom, however, I naturally understand not its mere form, forced down as from above, measured and controlled by the state, this eternal lie which, in reality, is nothing but the privilege of the few founded upon the slavery of all. Nor do I mean that "individualistic," selfish, petty, and *mock* freedom, which is propagated by J.J. Rousseau and all other schools of bourgeois liberalism. The mock freedom which is limited by the supposed right of all, and defended by the state, and leads inevitably to the destruction of the rights of the individual. No: I mean the only true freedom, that worthy of the name; the liberty which consists therein for everyone to develop all the material, intellectual, and moral faculties which lie dorment in him; the liberty which knows and recognises no limitations beyond those which nature decrees. In this sense, there are no limitations, for the laws of our own nature are not forced upon us by a law-giver who, beside or above us, sits on a throne. They are in us, the real basis of our bodily and intellectual existence. Instead of limiting them, we must know that they are the real condition and first cause of our liberty.

I mean that liberty of each which is not limited or restrained or curtailed by the liberty of another, but is strengthened and enlarged through it: the unlimited liberty of each through the liberty of all, liberty through solidarity, liberty in equality. (Political, & economical and social.) The liberty which has conquered brute force and vanquished the principle of authority, which is, always, only the expression of that force. The liberty, which will abolish all heavenly and earthly idols, and erect a new world of fellowship and human solidarity on the ruins of all states and churches.

I am a confirmed disciple of *economic and social equality*. Outside of this, I know, freedom, justice, manliness, morality, and the welfare of the individual as well as that of the community, can only be a hollow lie, an empty phrase. This equality must realise itself through the free organisation of labour and the voluntary cooperative ownership of the means of production, through the combination of the productive workers into freely organised communes, and the free federation of the communes. There must be no controlling intervention of the state.

This is the point which separates, especially, the revolutionary socialists from the authoritarian i. e. marxian socialists. Both work for the same end. Both are out to create a new society. Both agree that the only basis of this new society shall be: the organisation of labour which each and all will have to perform under equal economic conditions, following the demands of nature; and the common ownership of, everything that is necessary to perform that labour, lands, tools, machinery, etc. But, where as, the revolutionary socialists believe in the direct initiative of the workers themselves through their industrial combinations, this is anarchist stand point in contradiction to marxian or as it claims to be scientific. The authoritarians believe in the direct initiative of the state. They imagine they can reach their goal with the help of the radical parties (now it should be understood as communist) through the development and organisation of the political power of the working-class, especially the proletariat of the big towns, due to concentration of large industries employing large mass of proletariat. But the revolutionary socialists oppose all these compromising and confusing alliances. They are convinced that the goal of a free society can only be reached through the development and organisation of the non-political, but social power of the working class of both town and country, with the fusion of forces of all those members of the upper class who are willing to declass themselves and ready to break with the past, and to combine together for the same demands. The revolutionary socialists are opposed, therefore, to all politics.

Thus we have two methods:—

1) The organisation of the representative or political strength of the proletariat for the purpose of capturing political power in the state in order to transform society.

2) The organisation of the direct strength, the social and industrial solidarity of the proletariat for the purpose of abolishing all political power and the state.

The advocates of both methods believe in science, which is out to slay superstition, and which shall take the place of religious church belief. But the former propose to force it into humanity, whilst the latter seek ot convince the people of its truth, to educate them everywhere, so that they shall voluntarily organise and combine—freely, from the bottom upwards through individual initiative and according to their true interests, but never according to a plan drawn up before hand for the "ignorant masses" by a few intellectually superior persons.

Revolutionary—now known as libertarian socialists beleive that in the instictive yearnings and true wants of the masses, is to be found much sound reason and logic than in the deep wisdom of all the doctors, servants, and teachers of humanity who, after many disastrous attempts, still dabble in the problem of making the people happy. Humanity, think they, has been ruled and governed much too long and so they think this state of the affairs should continue. Indeed the source of people's trouble, lies not in this or that form of government, but in the existence and manifestation of Government itself, whatever form it may assume.

This is the historical difference between the authoritarian communist ideas, scientifically developed through the German Marxist school and partly adopted by English and American Socialists, on one hand and the Anarchist ideas of Joseph Pierre Proudhon which have educated the proletariat of the Latin countries and led them intellectually to the last consequences of Proudhon's teachings. This latter revolutionary or libertarian socialism has now for the first time, attempted to put its ideas into practice in the Paris Commune.

I am a follower of the Paris Commune, which, though dastardly murdered and drowned in blood by the assassins of the clerical and monarchial reaction, yet lives, more than ever, in the imagination and hearts of the European proletariat. I am its follower, especially because of the fact that it was a courageous, determined, negation of the state. It is a fact of enormous significance, that this should have happened in France, hitherto the land of strongest political centralisation; that it was Paris, the head and creator of this great cenralisation, which made the start— thus destroying itself and proclaiming with joy its fall, in order to give life to France, to Europe, to the whole world; thus revealing to all enslaved people—and who are the people who are not slaves—the only way to liberty and happiness; delivering a deathly stroke against the political traditions of bourgeois liberalism, and giving a sound basis to revolutionary socialism.

Paris thus earned for itself the curses of the reactionaries of France and Europe. It inaugurated the new era that of the final and entire liberation of the people, and their truly realised solidarity, above and in spite of all limitations of the State. Proclaimed the religion of humanity. Made manifest its humanism and atheism, and substituted the great truths of social, life and science for godly lies. Paris, heroic, sane, unflinching, asserted its strong belief in the future of humanity. It substituted liberty, justice, and fraternity for the falsehood and injustice of religious and political morality. Paris, choked in the blood of its children, symbolised humanity crucified by the international united reaction of Europe at the direct inspiration of the churches and the high priests (Politicians) of injustice. The next international upheaval of humanity will be the resurrection of Paris.

Such is the true meaning and the beneficial and immeasurably important results of the two-months' existence and memorable fall of the Paris Commune. It lasted only a short time. It was hampered too much by the deadly war it had to wage against the Versailles reaction and Holy Alliance. Consequently, it was unable to work out its Socialist programme, even theoretically, much less practically. The majority of the members of the Commune, even, were not Socialists in the real sense of the word. And if they acted as Socialists, it was only because they were irresistibly carried away by the nature of their surroundings, the necessity of their position, and not by their own innermost convictions. The Socialists, led by our friend Varlin, formed in the Commune only a disappearingly small minority, say fourteen or fifteen members. The rest consisted of Jacobins. But we must discriminate between Jacobins and Jacobins.

There are doctrinaire Jacobins like Gambetta whose,

oppressing lust for power and formal republicanism has lost the old revolutionary fire, and preserved only a respect for centralised unity and authority. This was the Jacobinism that betrayed the France of the people to the Prussian conquerors, and then to the native reaction. But there were honest revolutionary Jacobins also, the last heroic decendants of the democratic impulse of 1793, men and women who could sacrifice their centralised unity and well-armed authority to the needs of the revolution, rather than bend their conscience before the obnoxious reaction. In the vanguard of these great-hearted jacobins we see Deleeluse, a great and noble figure. Before everything he desired the triumph of the revolution; and as, without the people, no revolution is possible, as the people are Socialistically inclined, and could not be won for any other revolution than a social or economic one, Delecluse and his fellow honest Jacobins allowed themselves to be carried away by the logic of the revolutionary movement. Without desiring it, they became revolutionary Socialists, and signed proclamations and appeals whose general spirit was of a decidedly Socialist nature.

But, in spite of their honesty and goodwill, their Socialism was the product of external circumstances rather than inner conviction. They had neither the time nor the ability to overcome bourgeois prejudices diametrically opposed to their newly acquired Socialism. This internal conflict of opinion weakened them in action. They never got beyond fundamental theories, and were unable to come to decisive concusions such as would have severed their connection with bourgeois society once and for all.

This was a great calamity for the Commune and for the men themselves. It paralysed them, and they paralysed the Commune. But we must not reproach them on that account. Man does not change in a day, and we cannot change our natures and customs overnight. The Jacobins of the commune have shown their honesty by suffering themselves to be murdered for it. Who can expect more of them?

Even the people of Paris, under whose influence they thought and acted, were Socialists more by instinct than by well-balanced conviction. All their yearnings were in the highest degree entirely Socialistic. But their thoughts were expressed in traditional forms for removed from this height. Among the proletariat of the French towns, and even of Paris, many Jacobins prejudices still remain. Many false ideas about the necessity of dictatorship and government still flourish. The worship of authority—the inevitable result of religious education, that eternal source of all evil, all degradation, all enslavement of peoples—has not yet been entirely removed from its midst. So much is this the case that even the most intelligent sons of the people, the self-conscious Socialists of that time, have not yet been able to free themselves from this superstition. Were one to dissect their minds, one would find the Jacobin, the believer in government, huddled together in a little corner, forsaken and almost lifeless, but not quite dead.

Besides, the position of the small minority of class conscious and revolutionary Socialists in the Commune was very difficult. They felt that they lacked the support of the mass of the Paris population. The organisation of the International Workers' Association was very imperfect, and it only had a few thousand members. With this backing, they had to fight daily against a Jacobin majority. And under what circumstances! Daily they had to find work and bread for several hundred thousand workers, to organise and arm them, and to guard aganist reactionary conspiracies. All in a town like Paris, beleagured, menaced with starvation, and exposed to all underhand attacks of the reaction which had established itself in Versailles by kind permission of the Prussian Conqueror. They were forced to create a revolutionary government and army in order to oppose Versailles government and army. They had to forget and violate the first principles of revolutionary Socialism, and organise themselves as a Jacobin reaction, in order to fight the monarchical and clerical reaction.

It is obvious that, under these circumstances, the Jacobins were the stronger party. They were in a majority and possessed superior political cunning. Their traditions and greater experience in the organisation of government gave them a gigantic advantage over the few genuine Socialists. But the Jacobins took little advantage of this fact; they did not strive to give to the uprising of Paris a distinctive Jacobin character, but allowed themselves to drift into a social revolution.

Many Socialists, very consequential in their theory, reproach our Paris comrades with not having acted sufficiently Socialistic, whilst the barkers of the bourgeois forces accused them of having been too loyal to the Socialist programme. We will leave the latter gentry on one side now, and endeavour to convince the stern theorists of the liberation of labour that they are unjust to our Paris brethren. Between the best thories and their practical realisation is a gigantic difference, which cannot be covered in a few days. Those of us who knew for instance, our friend Varlin—to mention only him whose death was certain—how strong, well cosidered, and deeprooted were the convictions of Socialism in him and his friends. They were men whose enthusiasm, honesty, and self-sacrifice nobody could doubt. Their very honesty make them suspicious of themselves, and they underestimated their strength and character in face of the titanic labour to which they were consecrating their life and thought. Besides, they had the right conviction that, in the social revolution—which in this, as in every other respect, is the direct opposite of political revolution—the deeds of the single leading personality nearly disappear, and the independent, direct action of the masses count as everything. The only thing which the more advanced can do is to work out, spread, and explain the ideas which suit the requirements and ideals of the people, and contribute to the national strength of the latter by working untiringly on the task of revolutionary organisation—nothing more. Everything else can and must be accomplished by the people themselves. Otherwise we would arrive at political dictatorship; that is, a re-instatement of the State, privilege, inequality, persecution; a re-establishment, by a long and roundabout way, of political, social, and econmic slavery.

Varlin and all his friends; like all true Socialists, and like the average worker who is born and bred amongst the people, experienced in highest degree this well-justified fear of the continued initiative of the same men, this distrust of the rule of distinguished personalities. Their uprightness caused them to turn this fear and suspicion as much against themselves as against others.

In opposition to the, in my opinion, entirely erroneous

idea of State Socialists, that a dictatorship or a constitutional assembly—that has emerged from a political revolution—can proclaim and organise the social revolution by laws and degrees, our Paris friends were convinced that it could only be brought about and developed through the independent and unceasing efforts of the masses and the groups. They were a thousand times right. Where is the head, however genial, or—if one speaks of the collective dictatorship of an elected assembly, even if it consists of several hundred uncommonly well educated people—where is the brain that is mighty and grasping enough to grasp the unending number and multitude of true interests, yearnings, wills, and requirements, the sum total of which constitute the collective will of the people? And who could invent a social organisation which would satisfy every man? Such an organisation would be nothing less than a torture-chamber, into which the more or less aggressive State would put unhappy society. This has always happened up to now. But the social revolution must make an end of this antiquated system of organisation. It must give back to the masses, the groups, communes, societies, even to every man and woman, their full and unrestricted liberty. It must abolish, once and for all, political power. The State must go. With its fall must disappear all legal rights, all the lies of various religions. For law and religion were always only the forced justification for priviliged outrages and established aggression.

It is clear that liberty can only be restored to mankind, and that the true interests of society, of all groups, all local organisations, as well as every single, being can be entirely satisfied entirely only when *all* States have been abolished.

All the so-called "common interests of society" which are supposed to be represented by the State, are in reality nothing else than the entire and continued suppression of the true interests of the districts, communes, societies, and individuals which are subservient to the State. They are an imagination, an abstract idea, a lie. Under the guise of this idea of representing common interests, the State becomes a vast slaughter-house or cemetery, wherein is slain all the living energy of the people.

But an abstract idea can never exist for itself and through itself. It has no feet with which to walk, no arms with which to work, no stomach in which to digest its slaughtered victims. The religious idea, God, represents, in reality, the self-evident and real interests of a privileged class, the clergy, who represent the earthly half of the God idea. The State, the political abstraction, represents as real and self-evident interests of the bourgeoisie. To-day, that class is the most important and practically only exploiting class, which is threatening to swallow up all other classes. Priesthood is developing gradually into a very rich and mighty minority, but is rather relegated and with poor majority. The same is true of the bourgeoisie. Its political and social organisations are every day making for a real ruling oligarchy, to whom a majority of more or less conceited and impoverished bourgeois creatures who are obliged to serve the almighty oligarchy as blind tools. This majority lives in a continuous illusion, and is, through the irresistible power of economic development, unavoidably and ever more pulled down to the ranks of the proletariat.

The abolition of Church and State must be the first and essential condition for the true liberation of society.

Only afterwards can and must society organise itself on a new basis. But not from the top downwards, after a more or less beautiful plan of a few experts or theorists, or on the strength of decrees of a ruling power, or through a universal-suffrage-elected Parliament. Such a proceeding would lead inevitably to the creation of a new ruling aristocracy, *i.e.*, a class who have nothing in common with the people. This class would exploit and bleed the people under the pretence of the common welfare, or in order to preserve the new State.

The organisation of the society of the future must and can be accomplished only from the bottom upwards, through the free federation and union of the workers into groups, unions, and societies, which will unite again into districts, communes, national communes, and finally form a great international federation. Only thus can be evolved the true vital order of liberty and happiness for all, the order which is not opposed to the interests of the individual or of society, but on the contrary strengthens the same and brings them into harmony.

It is said that the harmony and the solidarity between the interests of the individual and society can never be effected, because of an inherent antagonism. But if these interests never and nowhere did harmonise, up to now, it has been the fault of the State in sacrificing the interests of the majority of the people to the gain of a small privileged minority. This oft-mentioned opposition of personal and social interests is only a swindle and political lie, which originated through the religious and theological lie of the Fall—a dogma which was invented to degrade man and destroy his consciousness of his own value. Support was lent to this false idea of antagonism of interests by the speculation of the metaphysical philosophies. These are closely related to theology. Metaphysics over-look the fact that man is a social animal, however, and view society as a mechanical and wholly artificial conglomeration of individuals, who suddenly organise themselves on the basis of a secret or sacred compact out of their free will, or at the dictation of a higher power. Before coming together in this fashion, these individuals had boasted an eternal soul and lived in alleged unlimited liberty!

But when the metaphysicians, especially those who believe in the immortality of the soul, assert that men, outside society, are free beings, they maintain that men can enter into society only by denying their freedom and natural independence, and sacrificing both their personal and local interests. This denial and sacrifice of the ego becomes greater the more developed the society and the more complicated its organisation. From this viewpoint the State becomes the expression of individual sacrifice, which all have to bring to its altar. In the name of the abstract and outragious lie called "the common good," and "law and order" it imperils increasingly all—personal liberty, in the interests of the governing class it exclusively represents. Hence the State appears to us as an inevitable negation and destruction of all liberty, all personal, individual, and common interests.

Everything in the metaphysical and theological system follows and solves itself. Therefore the upholders of these systems are obliged to exploit the masses through the medium of Church and State. Whilst filling their pockets and satisfying all their filthy desires, they tell themselves that they work for the honour of God, the triumph of civilisation, and the eternal welfare of the proletariat.

But we revolutionary Socialists, who believe neither in God, nor yet in (absolute or unqualified) free will, nor yet in the immortality of the soul, we say that liberty, in its fullest sense, must be the goal of human progress.

Our idealistic opponents, the theologians and metaphysicians, take the abstract "liberty" as the foundation of their theories. It is then quite easy for them to draw the conclusion that slavery is the indisputable condition of human existence. We, who are in our empirical scientific theory, materialists, strive in practice for the triumph of a sane and noble idealism. We are convinced that the whole wealth of the intellectual, moral and material development of humanity, as well as its seeming independence, is due to the fact that man lives in society. Outside of society man would not only *not* have been free. He would not even have been capable of becoming a man, *i. e.*, a self-conscious being, capable of thought and speech. Thinking and working together lifted man out of his animal condition. We are absolutely convinced that the whole life of man is a social product. His interests, yearnings, needs, dreams, and even his foolishness, as well as his brutality, injustice, and actions, depending, seemingly, on free will, are only the inevitable results of forces at work in our social life. Men are not independent of each other, but each influences the other. We are all in continual co-relation with our neighbours and surrounding nature.

In nature itself this wonderful co-working and fitting together of events does not take place without a struggle On the contrary, the harmony of the elements is but the result of this continual struggle, which is the condition of all life and of movement. Both in nature and society order without struggle is the equivalent of death.

Order is possible and natural in world system only when the latter is a previously thought out arrangement imposed upon mankind from above. The Jewish religious imagination of a godly law-giver makes for unparalleled nonsense, and the negation not only of all order, but of nature itself. "The laws of nature" relate only to the goal of nature itself. The phrase is not true if used to mean laws decreed by an outside authority. For these "laws" are nothing else than the continual adaptation which is part of the evolution of things, of the working together of vastly different passing but real facts. The sum total of all action and interaction is what we call "nature." The thoughts and science of man observe these phenomena, controlled and experimented with them and finally united them into a system, the single parts of which are called "laws." But nature itself knows no laws. Nature acts unconsciously. In itself it demonstrates the unending difference of its necessarily appearing and self repeating phenomena. This is how, thanks to the inevitableness of activity, the common order can and does exist.

So with human society, which apparently develops against nature, but in reality goes hand in hand with the natural and inevitable development of things. Only the superiority of man over the rest of the animals and his highly developed thinking ability brought a special feature into his evolution—also, by the way, quite natural since man, like everything else, is the material result of the working together and union of natural forces. This special feature is the calculating, thinking ability, the power of induction and abstraction. Through this man has been able to carry his thoughts outside himself, and so observe and criticise himself as a thing apart, some strange or foreign object. And as he, in his thoughts, lifts himself out of himself and the surrounding world, he arrives at the idea of the entire abstraction, the pure nothingness, the absolute. But this represents nothing beyond man's own ability to abstract thought, which looks down on all that is and finds peace in the entire negation of all that is. This is the very limit of the highest abstraction of thought: this is God.

Herein is to be found the spirit and historical proof of every theological and religious doctrine. Man did not understand nature and the material foundation of his own thoughts. He was unconscious of the natural circumstances and powers which were characteristic of them. So he failed to realise that his abstract ideas only expressed his own ability to abstract thought. Therefore, he came to regard the abstract idea as something really existing—something before which even nature sank into insignificance. And so he worshipped and honoured in every conceivable fashion this unreality of his imagination. But it became necessary to imagine more clearly and to make understood somehow this God, this supreme nothingness which seemed to contain all things in essence but not in fact. So primitive man enlarged his idea of God. Gradually he bestowed on the deity all the powers which existed in human society, good and bad, virtuous and vicious. Such was the beginning of all religions, such their evolution from fetish worship to Christianity.

We will not stop to analyse the history of religious, theological, and metaphysical nonsense, nor speak about the ever occurring godly incarnations and visions which have happened during centuries of human ignorance. Everyone knows that these superstitions occasioned terrible suffering, and their progress was acccompanied by rivers of blood and much mourning. All these terrible errors of poor humanity were inevitable in the evolution of society. They were the necessary effect, the natural consequence of that all powerful idea that the universe is governed and conditioned by a supernatural power and will. Century succeeds century. Man becomes more and more used to this belief. Finally it seeks to crush and to kill every effort towards any higher development.

The mad desire to rule or to govern, first on the part of a few men, then of a certain class, demanded that slavery and conquest should be accepted as the underlying principles of society. This, more than anything else, strengthened the terrible belief in a God above. Consequently, no social order could exist without being founded on the Church and State. All doctrinaires defend both of these outrageous institutions.

With their development increased the power of the ruling class, of the priests and aristocrats. Their first concern was to inoculate the enslaved peoples with the idea of the necessity, the benifit, and the sacredness of Church and State. And the purpose of all this was to change brutal and violent salvery into legal, divinely -pre-ordained and sanctified slavery.

Did the priests and aristocrats really and truly believe in these institutions which they were endeavouring to uphold with all their power, and to their own benefit? Or were they only lairs and hypocrites? In my opinion they were honest believers and dishonest deceivers simultaneously.

They themselves believed, since they participated, naturally, in the errors of the masses. Only later, at the time the old world declined—that is, in the Middle Ages, did they become unbelievers and shameless lairs. The founders of states can be regarded also as honest men. Man readily believes that which he desires and that which is not detrimental to his own interests. It makes no difference if he is intelligent and educated. Through his egotism and his desire to live with his neighbours and to profit by their estimation he will believe always only in that which is useful and desirable to him. I am convinced, for instance, that Thiers and the Versailles government were trying to convince themselves, violently, that they were saving France by murdering several thousand men, women, and children.

Even if the priests, prophets, aristocrats, and bourgeois of all times were honest believers, in spite of all, they were parasites. One cannot suppose that they believed every bit of nonsense in religion and politics which they taught the masses. I will not go so far back as to the time when two Augurs in Rome were unable to look into each others face without smiling. It is hard to believe that even in the time of mental darkness and superstition the inventors of miracles were convinced of their truth. The same may be said of politics, where the motto is: "One must understand how to govern and rob a people so that they do not complain too much or forget to be subservient, so that they get no chance to think of resentment and revolt."

How can one possibly believe after this that the men who make a business out of politics, and whose goal is injustice, violence, lies, treason, single, and wholesale murder, honestly believe that the wisdom and art of ruling the State make for the common weal? In spite of all their brutality they are not so stupid as to think this. Church and State were in all times the schools of vice. History testifies to their crimes. Ever and always were priest and politician the conscious, systematic, unyielding, bloodthirsty enemies and executioners of the people. But how can we reconcile two seemingly opposed things like cheater and cheated, liar and believer? In thought it looks difficult, but in life we find the two often together.

The great bulk of mankind live in a continual quarrel and apathetic misunderstanding with themselves. They remain unconscious of this, as a rule, until some uncommon occurrence wakes them up out of their sleep, and forces them to reflect on themslves and their surroundings.

In politics, as well as in religion, man is only a machine in the hands of his oppressors. But robber and robbed, oppressor and oppressed live side by side, ruled by a handful of people, in whom one recognises the real oppo- ressors. It is always the same type of men, who, free of all political and religious prejudice, consciously torture and oppress the rest of the people. In the 17th and 18th century, until the advent of the great revolution, they ruled Europe and did as they liked. They do the same to-day. But we have reason to hope that their rule will be over soon.

History teaches us that the chief priests of Church and State or also the sworn servants and creatures of these damnable institutions. Whilst consciously deceiving the people and leading them into disaster, these persons are concerned to uphold zealously the sanctity and unapproachability of both establishments. The Church, on the authority of all priests and most politicians, is essential to the proper care of the people's souls; and the State is indispensable, in their opinion, for the proper maintenance of peace, order, and justice. And the doctrinaires of all schools exclaim in chorus: "Without Church or Government, progress and civilisation is impossible."

We make no comment on the heavenly hereafter, since we do not believe in an immortal soul. But we are convinced that nothing offers a greater menace to truth and the progress of humanity than the Church. How else could it be? Is it not the task of the Church to chloroform the women and children? Does she not kill all sound reason and science with her dogmas, and degrade the self-respect of man by confusing his ideas of right and justice? Does she not preach eternal slavery to the masses in the interest of the ruling and oppressing class? And is she not determined to perpetuate the present reign of darkness, ignorance, misery, and crime? *For the progress of our age not to be an empty dream, it must first sweep the Church out of its path.*

APPENDIX I.

Bakunin's literary legacy is small. The man had no literary ambitions. He was too much of a social revolutionist, too genuine, to wish to stoop to literature. To play at depicting wrong where one should aim at destroying wrongs; to substitute words for action, art for life: this was no work for a full-grown labourer in the cause of bread and freedom. With Bakunin, writing was but a tool not an achievement. Words were the means to accomplishment itself. His purpose was other than that of writing. He wrote as he studied and observed—in order to answer questions of the day. He wrote under the pressure of some crisis in social struggle. And all his writings originated in the same realistic, direct, useful, unpremeditated way. To this fact they owe much of their unevenness and repetition. Bakunin's vitality, desire for action, and counsel to action, overflowed into writing. In this way, his essays and pamphlets arose.

As a rule, Bakunin sat down to write a letter to a friend dealing with some question of the movement. But the letter quickly grew to the size of a pamphlet, and the pamphlet to that of a book. The greatness of the urge, the impelling idea, caused the author to write so fluently; illustrations flowed so easily from his vast reservoir of contemporary knowledge; and he had so clear and complete a conception of the philosophy of history to illumine his vision, that the pages soon filled themselves. The theme developed easily, embellished with countless digressions, a veritable encyclopedia review. But always incomplete, always unfinished.

Bakunin was acquainted with Herzen, Ogareff, Mazzini, Ledru-Rollin and others. He participated in the uprising of 1848-1849, the Polish insurrection of the early sixties, and the secret Italian movements. He foresaw the fall of the French Empire and an upheaval in Paris. Thoughts, conceptions, facts and arguments borrowed from the realities of a period of struggle, invaded Bakunin's spirit and took possession of his being. His generalisation of historical philosophy, leading to revolutionary negation of class society, was richly adorned with facts and wisdom gathered from contemporary reality. This explains how, with all his errors, Bakunin stands out in working class history as "the fiercest representative of the idea of real revolutionary action."

Bakunin was unquestionably inferior to Marx as a political economist. His economics are Marxist, and he subscribed enthusiastically to Marx's theory of surplus value and dissection of the Capitalist system. Bakunin believed in the materialistic conception of history even more thoroughly than Marx. But when Marx, contrary to the logic of his own writing, began to play with Parliamentarism; when Marxism was proclaimed as *the only scientific socialism* at a time when it was becoming a theology and a metaphysic rather than a science; when Marxism degraded itself into a dull political class society electioneering, then Bakunin proclaimed his anti-Marxism in opposition to the negation of Socialist thought in action.

To Bakunin, exploitation and oppression were more than economic and political grievances. Hence, a fairer distribution of wealth, even if possible under the system, and a seeming participation in political power (democracy) were "remedies" that did not meet the situation. Democracy was not the cure for poverty but only the perpetuation of the disease. Democracy as understood and practised then was capitalistic and as such was the criminal perpetuation of poverty. Bakunin saw clearly that there was one problem only: economic exploitation and submission was connected intimately with all forms of *authority*, religious, political and social: and this *authority* was embodied in the *State*. Hence *Anarchism*, the negation of authority, the negation of priestcraft, was the essential factor in all real Socialism. To Bakunin, *Anarchism* defined *Socialism* as Submission defined Capitalism.

Bakunin did not confound "Government" with "Administration." He did not confuse the "State" with "Society". He did not pretend to believe in "Community" interest in a class society. He opposed class society and all its hypocritical masquerades. He proclaimed the need for freedom and defined Socialism as the proletarian determination to revolt to realise freedom. Thus, Bakunin opposed Anarchism to Parliamentarism. Mental, personal and social freedom are to him inseparable—*Atheism, Anarchism, Socialism*, an organic unit. His Atheism is not that of the ordinary Freethinker, who may be an authoritarian and an anti-Socialist; nor is his Socialism that of a parliamentarian, albeit Marxist, who may be, and very often claims to be, an Authoritarian and a Christian, or speaks as though he were both; but his Atheism and Socialism complete each other. They interpenetrate and constitute a living realisation of freedom, a social condition of happiness. This thoroughness makes Bakunin's Socialist propaganda unique.

If Proudhon's vision was blurred by a kind of bourgeois

pacifism, Marx certainly sacrificed his own revolutionary understanding for political and personal dictatorship. He liquidated his great revolutionary work in an unscrupulous vanity and an all-consuming miserable pretension to absolute priesthood that knew no bounds. But for his desire to dominate, Marx would have been the great working class emancipator. His mighty mind descended to petty spleen because his will could brook no qualifying influences. Marx was his world—and his limitation. This self-immolation of a great intellect to a narrow will was nothing less than a terrible disease from which Marx suffered. It reduced a prophet to a priest and a great movement to an impotence. It made Marx less than a political revolutionist, a mere parliamentary temporiser, where the mind of the man visioned and understood and cried out for the complete social revolution. Not even when one considers the long line of Labour Judas Iscariots M.P.'s, is it possible to discover one person in the history of the workers' struggle who sold his birth right for a more miserable mess of pottage than Karl Marx. For he lived and died in poverty. He shared all the misery of the struggle. Only his semi disciples, the disciples of his error and not his vision, prospered into defenders of Capitalism. They praised him for his confusion and his name grew to shaded mediocre respectability. Whereas he was intended to be the symbol of proletarian challenge, the enemy of Capitalism.

As early as July, 1848, possibly because Bakunin saw good in Proudhon as well as in Marx, the latter's *Neue Rheinische Zeitung* accused Bakunin of being a paid spy in the employ of the Russian Ambassador. Marx's paper added that George Sand, the novelist, possessed papers that would establish the charge. Bakunin appealed to George Sand to clear his name of this odious accusation, and she wrote to the *Zeitung* :

"The facts related by your correspondent are absolutely false. I never had any documents which contained insinuations against M. Bakunin. I never had any reason, or authority, to express any doubts as to the loyalty of his character and the sincerity of his views. I appeal to your honour and to your conscience to print this letter in your paper immediately."

Marx published this letter with the explanation that, in publishing the charge, the *Zeitung* had given Bakunin an opportunity to dispel a suspicion long current in certain Parisian circles. In September, 1853, Marx had to repudiate this charge against Bakunin in the columns of the London *Morning Post*.

Marx knew that, at the International Congress at Basle, in 1869, Bakunin demanded an investigation of the charge from Wilhelm Liebknecht. He was vindicated completely and Liebknecht publicly apologised.

Yet, in a "confidential communication" sent to the Brunswick Committee, through Kugelmann, Marx wrote of Bakunin:—

"Bakunin......found opponents there who not only would not allow him to exercise a dictatorial influence, but also said he was a Russian Spy."

Lafargue bitterly attacked Bakunin and his comrades from 1872 onwards. Yet his enmity was not sufficient to please the concentrated vindictiveness of his father-in-law. On November 11th, 1882, Marx wrote to Engels:—

o. "Longuet, the last Proudhonist, and Lafargue, the last Bakuninist ! May the Devil come to fetch them !"

How different was the attitude of Bakunin !

Early in the summer of 1848, Bakunin quarrelled with Marx and Engels over Herwegh's plan to invade Germany with armed legions. Writing of this quarrel in 1871, Bakunin confessed:—

"On this subject, when I think of it now, I must say frankly that Marx and Engels were right. They truly estimated the affairs of those days."

The International Working Men's Association was founded at St. Martin's Hall, London, on September, 29th, 1864, to unite and weld together all workers who would come together to work for their emancipation from Capitalism, irrespective of the shades of opinion on principles and tactics which divided them. This broad principle was respected for five years. The Congress held at Basle, Switzerland, in September, 1869, was the last conference at which Marxists, Revolutionary Collectivists or Anarchists, Proudhonian Mutualists, Trade Unionists, Co-operators and social reformers met in fair discussion and tried to elaborate lines of common action, useful and acceptable to all. [The Congress of 1868-1869 showed that Anti-Parliamentarism was spreading through the sections of the international owing to Bakunin's influence. This was mortifying to Marx, who, despite the Anti-Parliamentary logic of his thought and writings, worked, through the London General Council of the Association, for the development of parliamentarism.]

Owing to the Franco-Prussian War, no congress was held in 1870, and in 1871. Marx convened a private congress in London, September 17-23, 1871. At this congress or conference Marx, although such conduct was contrary to the opinion he had developed in his *Civil War in France*, struck the blow he must have premeditated from some time, namely, the enforcement of parliamentarism. He imposed upon the Association the official doctrine of political action, which meant Labour Parties, electioneering, the practical Administration of Capitalism, and the steady negation of Socialism.

The Marxist Parliamentary London Conference caused the Jurassian Federation to convene an Anti-Parliamentary Conference at Sonvillier, Switzerland, on November the 12th, protesting against the parliamentary doctrine being imposed on the International, and calling for a General Congress. The circular issued by these sections was known as the Sonvillier Circular. Marx replied to this circular in a recriminating document, to which he affixed the names of the members of the General Council, called *On The Pretended Split in the International*. This was dated March 5th, 1872. It was printed and circulated in May, 1872. Bakunin and others replied to it in the Jura *Bulletin* of June 15th, 1872.

It is quite true that the Marxist Congress was convened at the Hague in September, 1872: and that a few days later Bakunin and his comrades convened an Anti-Parliamentary Congress at St. Imier. This Congress met on September 13th, and accepted the rules and principles of the secret society, the Alliance of Revolutionary Socialists, that Bakunin had drawn up at Zurich since August 30th, 1872. It is true also that whilst the Marxist General Council at New York simply abolished the International, the Anti-Parliamentarians and

Anarchists reorganised the Association *on the basis of St. Mier priniciples*, and convened a Congress at Geneva (September. 1873), and further Congresses at Brussels, Berne and Veniers. But virtually the International was dissolved. One does not identify the Anarchist propaganda that resulted from these conferences with Anti-Parliamentarism, necessarily. Rather this Anarchism merely balanced the Parliamentarism that came into existence. Anti-Parliamentarism regards both as parodies of the real struggle. It does not share the Anarchist objection to abstract authority: it does not make the state the author of economic society: it does believe in the class struggle: it does negate political society: it does stand for the liquidation of political and property society in industrial and useful society.

From this period of activity (1848-1873), Anti-Parliamentarism accepts, not uncritically, but gladly, though critically, all Marx's writings of importance: his *Communist Manifesto* (as he suggested correcting it); *Eighteenth Brumaire;* and the *Civil War in France; Revolution and Counter-Revolution; The Poverty of Philosophy.* The Anti-Parliamentary movement has not the same interest in Marx's *Eastern Question*. But it grounds its teaching on *Capital* and *Wage-Labour and Capital*. As a movement, we would say that Anti-Parliamentarism has not such regard for *Value, Price, and Profit*. Personally, we consider this work unsatisfactory and intended to justify palliation and reform. Opinion is divided as to its worth but, except for an odd paragraph, it is an elaborate joke, an attempted repudiation of Marxist logic written by Marx in the same spirit, and to the same end, as Lenin wrote his *Infantile Sickness of the Left-Wing*.

Anti-Parliamentarism accepts gratefully most of

Bakunin's writings. Unlike the Anarchist disciples of Bakunin, it makes Bakunin's criticism of *The Paris Commune and the State idea,* in political and working class usefulness, below Marx's *Civil War in France.* Anti-Parliamentarism endorses Bakunin's healthy opposition to the God Idea, i. e. the deification of the abstract General Idea.

Whilst agreeing, in the main, with the Marxists in their distinction between Scientific and Utopian Socialism, Anti-Parliamentarism does not believe in ihe neglect of the Utopian Socialists. Anti-Parliamentarians believe that St. Simon, for example, clearly understood the trend of Social development towards industrial Society. It believes that much of the Utopian thought should be embodied in the current literature of the working class movement and not discarded ruthlessly. Nor is Anti-Parliamentarism impressed with the intrigues, the pedantry, the abstractions, the electioneerings, and the capitalist loyalties of "Scientific Socialism." In the main, the practical history of "Scientific Socialism" has been a record, neither of Science nor yet of Socialism.

Anti-Parliamentarism does not endorse Proudhon. But it believes that, on the question of the revolutionary development and the evolution of the revolutionary idea, Proudhon's *Revolutionary Idea* is a wonderful and useful work and ranks with the writings of Marx as a classic. On the subject of the liquidation of military and political society, Proudhon writes usefully and scientifically and holds a place, therefore, in the ranks of pioneers of Anti-Parliamentarism. The Anti-Parliamentarians are opposed to Proudhon being dismissed with contempt under the mistaken idea that such dismissal is an expression of revolutionary thought.

Marx: Proudhon: Bakunin: dead, their private feuds forgotten: their errors noted and over-ruled by time: are the three great founders of Anti-Parliamentary thought and action and the harbringers of the New Social Order of usefulness, wealth, health and freedom.

APPENDIX II.

Herzen, as has been stated, was the natural son of rich nobleman named Iakavlev and of a Stuttgardt lady, Louise Haaag. Herzen's name was a fancy one and signified a love token. "Herzen's kind" means "child of the heart." His father spared no expense in the matter of his education. The result was that Herzen not merely spoke correctly but brilliantly in Russian, French, English, and German. Despite these advantages he appealed to a Russian audience only. In 1865 he met Garibaldi in London. The effect of this meeting was to convince Herzen that, as Garibaldi was the Italian patriot, he must prove himself a Russian one. Unlike Herzen, Bakunin demanded the European stage. He remained the Slav at heart and before the audience of International Labour paraded his hatred of the Teuton. The Germans, he declared, were authoritarians. Their socialism was a menace. Despite phrases of equality and justice, they would bring the workers of the world to disaster. At heart the Teuton was a counter-revolutionist. He would change; but it would require half-a-century of falsehood and illusion ending in debacle before he would be converted to real communism and realise the need of revolutionary struggle.

Bakunin outlined the case against Germany, and enunciated his theory of the historic mission of the French, in his "Letters to a Frenchman About the Present Crisis" and his pamphlet on "The Knouto Germanic Empire." He disowned nationalism and declared that patriotism was a very mean, narrow, and interested passion. It was fundamentally inhuman and conserved exploitations and privileges. It was fostered by the Napoleons, Bismarcks, and Czars in order to destroy the freedom of nations. By a strange turn of thought and twist of the pen Bakunin proceeded from this reasoning to deduce an argument for French patriotism as opposed to German. He said:—

> "When the masses become patriotic they are stupid, as are to-day a part of the masses of Germany, who let themselves be slaughtered in tens of thousands, with a silly enthusiasm, for the triumph of that great unity, and for the organisation of that German Empire, which, if founded on the ruins of usurped France, will become the tomb of all hopes of the future."

It may be that Bakunin was visioning the future correctly. Much of his prophecy about the period of reaction that must follow in the wake of parliamentary socialism has been justified. The subjection of the French proletariat to the demands of Napoleon III. was not the correct revolutionary answer to Prussian militarism. It was the continuation of militarism and the surrender of socialism to reaction. The problem may have been difficult. It was Bakunin's business to find a correct revolutionary answer or else to keep silent. Instead, he shaved history shamefully so as to oppose the France of 1793 to the Germany of Bismarck. The France of Napoleon, of Bourbon royalism and of bourgeoisie republicanism was dismissed from view ... He pictured the world as waiting on the intiation of France for its advance towards liberty, equality and fraternity. France was to drive back Germany, exile her traitor officials and inaugurate socialism. Said Bakunin:-

> "What I would consider a great misfortune for the whole of humanity would be the defeat and death of France as a great national manifestation: the death of its great national

> character, the French spirit; of the courageous, heroic instincts, of the revolutionary daring, which took with storm, in order to destroy, all authorities that had been made holy by history, all power of heaven and earth. If that great historical nature called France should be missed at this hour, if it should disappear from the world scene; or—what would be much worse—if the spirited and developed nature should fall suddenly from the honoured height which she has attained, thanks to the work of heroic genius of past generations—into the abyss, and continue her existence as Bismarck's slave: a terrible emptiness will engulf the whole world. It would be more than a national catastrophe. It would be a worldwide misfortune, a universal defeat."

It is only necessary to add that Bakunin had to attack the great "French spirit" that murdered in cold blood the Communards in the May-June days of 1871. On the other side, Marx, who also eulogised the Communards, had declared for the German spirit of order and saw in the French disaster not so much the defeat of Napoleon III. or the triumph of the Prussian Kaiser but the defeat on the international field of thought of Proudhon and the triumph of Marx. These Gods! How they nod!

Bakunin believed in the Russian nationalism, bound on the east by the Tartars, and on the west by the Germans. This meant believing in the German nation, bounded on the west by France, and on the east by Russia. It meant the status quo. He was upholding the States of Europe. Yet he wrote: —

> "Usurpation is not only the outcome, but the highest aim of all states, large or small, powerful or weak, despotic or liberal, monarchic, aristocratic or democratic......It follows that the war of one State upon another is a necessity and common fact, and every peace is only a provisional truce."

This idea was not worked out at some other time,

under different circumstances, but in these "Letters to a Frenchman" eulogising the national spirit. He asserted that all States were bad, and there could be no virtuous State:—

"Who says State, says power, oppression, exploitation, injustice—all these established as the prevailing system and as the fundamental conditions of the existing society. The State never had a morality, and can never have one. Its only morality and justice is its own advantage, its own existence, and its own omnipotence at any price. Before these interests, all interests of mankind must disappear. The State is the negation of mankind."

"So long as there is a State, war will never cease. Each State must overcome or be overcome. Each State must found its power on the weakness, and, if it can, without danger to itself, on the abrogation of other States. To strive for an International justice and freedom and lasting peace, and therewith seek the maintenance of the State, is a ridiculous naivete."

Bakunin had to escape this very charge of ridiculous naivete.

Bakunin closed his stormy career at Berne, on the 1st July, 1876. He had founded the social democratic alliance and been expelled from the Marxist International. It was decided at his funeral to reconcile the social democrats and the anarchists in one association. Fraternal greetings were exchanged between the Jura federation, assembled at Chaux-de-Fonds, and the German social democratic congress at Gotha. At the eighth international congress, at Berne, in October, the social democrats and the anarchists met and expressed the desire that all socialists should treat each other with mutual consideration and complete common understanding. A banquet concluded this congress. Caferio, the disciple of Bakunin, drank to Marxism and the German socialists. De Paepe, the Marxist, toasted the memory of Bakunin. All

Bakunin's fiery words against the State, his talk of the revolution, his hurrying across Europe to boost first one and then another insurrection had ended seemingly in vapour, smoke! All Marx's insurrectional politics, his opposition to the parliamentary joint stock republic, his faith in the Commune and not the empire, seemed vanities. Marx was not reconciled with Bakunin at these conferences. The fundamental revolutionary inspiration of both were made subsidiary to the parliamentary ideas of Lassalle, from whom the social democrats drew their fatal inspiration. Since the days of the Commune the slogan of Lassalle, "Through universal suffrage to victory," has been substituted for Marx's magnificent: "Workers of all lands, unite! You have nothing to lose but your chains! You have a world to gain!"

"To set about to make a revolution," said Lassalle, "is the folly of immature minds, which have no notion of the laws of history." Thus he interpreted the events of 1848 as an argument for direct universal suffrage. Thus his disciples interpretated the events of 1871. Believing that it understood the laws of history the European social democracy buried socialism and attempted to murder outright the European proletariat in the world war of 1914 to 1918. The war ended, it had given birth to Fascism. With this hopeless movement of middle-class suffrage, the anarchists seriously thought of identifying themselves. They imagined such an alliance to be an honour to Bakunin, just as the Marxists thought they were honouring Marx by repudiating his revolutionary principles.

"And so you think that Marx and Bakunin were at one," said my friend.

"Yes," I replied, "I think that they were at one. I believe that they were one in purpose and in aspiration. But they accomplished distinct tasks and served different functions. It would not do for us all to act the same part. Fitted by temperament to enact a peculiar role, each man felt his work to be a special call, the one aim of life. This developed strong personality. And when the two strong personalities came into conflict through the nature of their respective tasks, the natural antagonisms of their temperament displayed themselves. Then came fools, who called themselves disciples of the wise men, and magnified their accidental collisions into vital discords of purpose. Do we not know the friend who persuades us to quarrel? And do we not know the 'disciples' who are actually street brawlers of a refined order? Marx and Bakunin have suffered at the hands of these mental numskulls.

"But how would you define the difference between the two men," pursued my friend.

"Very easily," I answered, "Marx DEFINED the Social Revolution, whilst Bakunin EXPRESSED it. The first stood for the invincible logic of the cause. The second concentrated in his own person its unquenchable spirit. Marx was an impregnable rock of first principles, remorselessly composed of facts. He dwarfed the intelligence of Capitalist society and witnessed to the indestructability of Socialism. He incarnated the proletarian upheaval. He was the immovable mountain of the revolution. Bakunin, on the other hand, was the tempest. He symbolised the coming flood. Both were great brave men; and together they gave completeness to the certitude of revolution. They promised success by land and by water. They symbolised inexhaustible patience, unwearying stability, inevitable growth, and tireless, resistless attack. Who can conceive of a world not made up of land and water? Who can conceive of the Social Revolution without the work of **Marx** and Bakunin?

But my friend was not convinced; so we turned to other subjects.

APPENDIX III.

Many comrades have found it hard to understand the difference between Marx and Bakunin. The story is very simple and can be told clearly.

During his imprisonment and exile, Bakunin was attacked by Marx and the latter's friends. Bakunin summarised the attack:—

> "While I was having a far from amusing time in German and Russian fortresses, and in Siberia, Marx and Co. were peddling, clamouring from the housetops, publishing in English and German newspapers, the most abominable rumours about me. They said that it was untrue to declare that I had been imprisoned in a fortress, that, on the contrary, Czar Nicholas had received me with open arms, had provided me with all possible conveniences and enjoyments, that I was able to amuse myself with light women, and had an abundance of champagne to drink. This was infamous, but it was also stupid."

After Bakunin arrived in London, in 1861, and settled down to his work on Herzen's *Kolokol*, an English newspaper published a statement by a man named Urquhart, declaring that Bakunin had been sent by the Czar to act as a spy. Bakunin challenged his calumniator and heard no more of the matter.

In November, 1864, Bakunin had an interview with Marx in London. Bakunin described the interview in the following terms:—

> "At that time I had a little note from Marx, in which he asked me whether he could come to see me the next day. I answered in the affirmative, and he came. We had an explanation. He said that e had never said or done anything against me; that, on the

contrary, he had always been my true friend, and had retained great respect for me. I knew that he was lying, but I really no longer bore any grudge against him. The renewal of the acquaintanceship interested me morover, in another connection. I knew that he had taken a great part in the foundation of the International. I had read the manifesto written by him in the name of the provisional General Council, a manifesto which was weighty, earnest, and profound, like everything that came from his pen when he was not engaged in personal polemic. In a word, we parted outwardly, on the best of terms, although I did not return his visit."

Writing to Engels, under date, November 4, 1864, Marx says:—

"Bakunin wishes to be remembered to you. He has left for Italy to-day. I saw him yesterday evening once more, for the first time after sixteen years. He said that after the failure in Poland he should, in future, confine himself to participation in the Socialist Movement. On the whole he is one of the few persons whom I find not to have retrogressed after sixteen years, but to have developed further. I had a talk with him also about Urquhart's denunciations."

Bakunin wanted to be on good terms with Marx, for the sake of building up the International. He desired to devote himself henceforward exclusively to the Socialist Movement. This was difficult because of Marx's injustice. Bakunin tells the story thus:—

"In the year 1848, Marx and I had a difference of opinion, and I must say that he was far more in the right of it than I. In Paris and Brussels he had founded a section of German Communists, and had, in alliance with the French and a few English Communists, supported by his friend and inseperable comrade, Engels, founded in London the first international association of Communists of various lands.........I, myself, the fumes of the revolutionary movement in Europe having gone to my head, had been much more interested in the negative than in the positive side of this revolution, had been, that is to say, much more concerned with the overthrow of the extant than with the question of the upbuilding and organisation of what was to follow. But there was one point in which I was right and he was wrong. As a Slav, I wanted the liberation of the Slav race from the German yoke. I wanted this liberation to be brought about by the revolution, that is to say by the destruction of the regime of Russia, Austria, Prussia, and Turkey, and by the re-organisation of the peoples from below upwards through their own freedom, upon the foundation of complete economic and social equality, and not through the power of any authority, however revolutionary it might call itself, and however intelligent it might in fact be.

"Already, at this date, the difference between our respective systems (a difference which now severs us in a way that, on my side, has been very carefully thought out) was well marked. My ideals and aspirations could not fail to be very displeasing to Marx. First of all, because they were not his own; secondly, because they ran counter to the convictions of the authoritarian Communists; and finally, because, being a German patriot, he would not admit then, any more than he does to-day, the right of the Slavs to free themselves from the German yoke—for still, as of old, he thinks that the Germans have a mission to civilise the Slavs, this meaning to Germanise them whether by kindness or force."

"To punish me for being so bold as to aim at realising an idea different from and indeed actually opposed to his, Marx then revenged himself after his own fashion. He was editor of the *Neue Rheinische Zeitung*, published in Cologne. In one of the issues of that paper I read in the Paris correspondence that Madame George Sand, with whom I had formerly been acquainted, was said to have told some one it was necessary to be cautious in dealing with Bakunin, for it was quite possible that he was some sort of Russian agent."

The *Morning Advertiser*, for September 1, 1853, published the statement by Marx that, on July 5, 1848, the *Neue Rheinische Zeitung* received two letters from Paris, declaring that George Sand possessed letters compromising Bakunin, "showing that he had recently been in communication with the Russian government." One was from the Havas Bureau, and the other from Dr. Ewerbeck, sometime leader of the Federation of the Just.

Bakunin described the effect of this accusation and his reaction to it :—

" The accusation was like a tile falling from a roof upon my head, at the very time when I was fully immersed in revolutionary organisation, and it completely paralysed my activities for several weeks. All my German and Slav friends fought shy of me. I was the first Russian to concern himself actively with revolutionary work, and it is needless for me to tell you what feelings of traditional mistrust were accustomed to arise in western minds when the words Russian revolutionist were mentioned. In the first instance, therefore, I wrote to Madame Sand."

Bakunin's life as an agitator, his insecurity of existence, his entire manner of living rendered it easy to undermine his prestige by sowing suspicion. This was also the policy of the Russian Embassy. In order to reply to Marx and the Czarist traducers, Bakunin wrote to George Sand. The text of George Sand's letter to the *Zei'ung*, dated August 3, 1848, is reproduced on page 5 of the Appendix I. Her declaration rehabilitated Bakunin as a revolutionary and a victim of slanderous conspiracy.

Slander never dies. In 1863, when he was about to enter Switzerland, a Basle paper declared that he had involved Polish refugees in disaster whilst remaining immune. German Socialist (sic) periodicals constantly slandered him. Marx never missed a chance of speaking against him.

Otto Ruhle has described how Marx wrote to a young Russian, seeking information regarding Bakunin. Marx was at his old trick of attempting to discredit Bakunin.

For reasons of conspiracy, Marx referred to Bakunin as *"my old friend Bakunin— I don't know if he is still my friend."* Marx persuaded too well: for his correspondent forwarded the letter to Bakunin. Marx complained of the result: *"Bakunin availed himself of the circumstances to excuse a sentimental entree."*

Ruhle comments—

"This sentimental entree not only redounded to Bakunin s credit, not only showed his good feeling and his insight, but deserved a better reception from Marx than the biting cynicism and the derogatory insolence which it was encountered (cynicism and insolence which were only masks for embarrassment)."

Bakunin wrote:—

"You ask whether I am still your friend. Yes, more than ever, my dear Marx, for I understand better than ever how right you were to walk along the broad road of the economic revolution, to invite us all to follow you, and to denounce all those who wandered off into the byways of nationalist or exclusively political enterprise. I am now doing what you began to do more than twenty years ago. Since I formally and publicly said good-bye to the bourgeois of the Berne Congress, I know no other society, no other milieu than the world of the workers. My fatherland is now the International, whose chief founder you have been. You see then dear friend, that I am your pupil—and I am proud to be this. I think I have said enough to make my personal position and feelings clear to you."

Bakunin met Marx with simplicity and friendship. Ruhle points out that Bakunin endeavoured honestly to be on good terms with Marx and to avoid friction. He adds that Bakunin loved the peasants and detested intellectualism and abstract systems, with their dogmatism and intolerance. He hated the modern State, industrialism, and centralisation. He had the most intense dislike for Judaism, which he considered loquacious, intriguing, and exploitative. All that authority and theorising for which he had an instinctive abhorrence were, for him, incorporated in Marx. He found Marx's self-esteem intolerable. Yet he mastered his spiritual repugnance and antagonism for the sake of building the movement of struggle towards Freedom, from loyalty to the workers, and from a sense of justice to Marx's worth as a master in the struggle. Bakunin's loyalty and aspiration after friendship were magnificent. It lent him a stature that dwarfs the envious and contemptible Marx into a mere pigmy. With justice Bakunin says of Marx and his political circle:—

"Marx loved his own person much more than he loved his friends and apostles, and no friendship could hold water against the silghtest wound to his vanity. He would far more readily forgive infidelity to his philosophical and socialist system.... Marx will never forgive a slight to his person. You must worship him, make an idol of him, if he is to love you in return; you must at least fear him, if he is to tolerate you. He likes to sorround him-self with pygmies, with lackeys and flatterers. All the same, there are some remarkble men among his intimates.

"In general, however, one may say that in the circle of Marx's intimates there is very little brotherly frankness, but a great deal of machination and diplomacy. There is a sort of tacit struggle, and a compromise between the self-loves of the various persons concerned: and where vanity is at work, there is no longer place for brotherly feeling. Every one is on his guard, is afraid of being sacrified, of being annihilated. Marx's circle is a sort of mutual admiration society. Marx is the chief distributor of honours, but is also invariably perfidious and malicious, the never frank and open, inciter to the persecution of those whom he suspects, or who have had the misfortune of failing to show all the veneration he expects.

"As soon as he has ordered a persecution, there is no limit to the baseness and infamy of the method. Himself a Jew, he has round him in London and in France and above all in Germany, a number of petty, more or less able, intriguing, mobile, speculative Jews (the sort of Jews you can find all over the place), commercial employees, bank clerks, men of letters, politicians, the correspondents of newspapers of the most various shades of opinion, in a word, literary go-betweens, just as they are financial go-betweens, one foot in the bank, the other in the Socialist Movement, while their rump is in German periodical literature ... These Jewish men of letters are adepts in the art of cowardly, odious, and perfidious insinuations. They seldom make open accusation, but they insinuate, saying they 'have heard—it is said—it may not be true, but,' and then they hurl the most abominable calumnies in your face."

Bakunin had a profound respect for Marx's intellectual abilities and scientific efficiency. When he read Marx's *Capital* he was amazed, and promptly set to work upon translating it into Russian. He translated *The Communist Manifesto* into Russian in 1862.

Writing to Herzen, Bakunin said :—

"For five-and-twenty years Marx has served the cause of Socialism ably, energetically, and loyally, taking the lead of every one in this matter. I should never forgive myself if, out of personal motives, I were to destroy or diminish Marx's beneficial influence. Still, I may be involved in a struggle against him, not because he has wounded me personally, but because of the State Socialism he advocates."

Bakunin describes how simple and personal was the cause of the struggle being renewed. He writes :—

"At the Peace Congress in Geneva, the veteran Communist, Becker, gave me the first, and as yet only, volume of the extremely importat, learned, profound, although very abstract work *Capital* Then I made a terrible mistake : I forgot to write Marx in order to thank him ... I did not hasten to thank him, and to pay him a compliment upon his really outstanding book. Old Philip Becker who had known Marx for a very long time, said to me, when he heard of this forgetfulness : 'What, you haven't written to him yet ? Marx will never forgive you' !"

Bakunin thought that his forgetfulness could be ranked as a personal slight and an unpardonable discourtesy. But he did not believe that it could lead to a resumption of hostilities. It did. Frau Marx wrote to Becker as follows:—

> "Have you seen or heard anything of Bakunin? My husband sent him, as an old Hegelian, his book — not a word or a sign. There must be somthing underneath this! One cannot trust any of these Russians; if they are not in the service of the Little Father in Russia, then they are in Herzen's service here, which amounts to much the same thing."

Bakunin was unable to persuade the Berne Congress of the League of Peace and Freedom to adopt a revolutionary programme and to affiliate to the International. He resigned, and in coujunction with Becker, founded the International Alliance of Social Revolutionaries. His aim was to affiliate the Alliance to the International. At this time, Bakunin's programme was somewhere between that of Marx and Proudhon.

Mehring describes Bakunin's place in relation to Marx as follows:—

> "Bakunin had advanced far beyond Proudhon, having absorbed a larger measure of European culture; and he understood Marx much better than Proudhon had done. But he was not so intimately acquainted with German philosophy as Marx, nor had he made so thorough a study of the class struggles of Western European nations. Above all, his ignorance of political economy was much more disastrous to him than ignorance of natural science had been to Proudhon. Yet he was revolutionary through and through; and like Marx and Lassalle, he had the gift of making people listen to him.
>
> "Marx favoured centralism, as manifested in the contemporary organisation of economic life and of the State; Bakunin favoured federalism, which had been the organisational principle of the precapitalist era. That was why Bakunin found most of his adherents in Italy, Spain, and Russia, in countries where capitalist development was backward. Marx's supporters, on the other hand, were recruited from

lands of advanced capitalist development, those with an industrial proletariat. The two men represented two successive phases of social revolution. Furthermore, Bakunin looked upon man rather as the subject of history who, 'having the devil in his body," spontaneously ripens for the revolution, and merely needs to have his chains broken; but Marx regarded man rather as the object, who must slowly be trained for action, in order that, marshalled for class activity, he may play his part as a factor of history. The two outlooks might have been combined, for in combination they supply the actual picture of man in history. But in the case of both of these champions, the necessary compromise was rendered impossible by the orthodox rigidity of intellectual dogmatism, by deficient elasticity of the will, and by the narrow circumstances of space and time, so that in actual fact they became adversaries. Then, owing to their respective temperaments, owing to the divergencies in mental structure which found expression in behaviour, their opposition in concrete matters developed into personal enmity."

Mehring defends Marx too eloquently. When we gaze at the world to-day, and the condition of the Labour Movement, we must feel that their was much more to be said for Bakunin's approach than for that of Marx.

Inspired by Marx, the General Council of the International refused to accept the affiliation of the Alliance. The affiliation was proposed by the Genevese section which was led by Bakunin.

Marx now denounced the Bakuninist programme as "an ollapodrida of worn-out commonplaces, thoughtless chatter; a rose-garland of empty motions, and insipid emprovisation."

Marx feared the influence of Bakunin among the homeworkers in the watchmaking industry of the Neuchatel and Bernese Jura. In 1865, Dr. Coullery had founded in La Chaux des Fonds, a section of the International. Its principal leader was James Guillaume, a teacher at the Industrial School in Le Locle. The Jura section was federalistically inclined and soon became ardent supporters of Bakunin. He amalgamated their groups into a federal council; founded a weekly, *Egalite* and started a vigorous revolutionary movement. In London this aroused the impression that Bakunin was trying to capture the International. At the Basle Congress of the International, on September 5 and 6, 1869, Bakunin was no longer, as he had been in Brussels, alone against the Marxian front, but was backed up by a resolute phalanx of supporters. It was obvious that Bakunin's influence was on the increase. This became especially plain during the discussion on the question of direct legislation by the people (initiative and referendum).

At this Congress, Bakunin once more brought to a head the slanders that the Marxists had circulated concerning him. His opponents had tried to check his influence by a flood of suspicions and invectives.

In 1868, the *Demokratisches Wokhenblatt*, published in Leipzig, under Wilhelm Liebknecht's editorship, attacked Bakunin's personal honour severely. At the same time, Bebel wrote to Becker, that Bakunin was "probably an agent of the Russian Government." Liebknecht declared that Bakunin was in the Czars' pay.

Bakunin secured the appointment of a court of arbitration to investigate the charges. Liebknecht had no proofs to adduce, and declared that his words had been misunderstood. The jury unanimously agreed that Liebknecht had behaved with "criminal levity," and made him give Bakunin a written apology. The adversaries shook hands before the Congress. Bakunin made a spill out of the apology, and lighted a cigarette with it.

Bakunin never tried to pay back Marx in the same coin. Mehring says of Bakunin's writings, that "we shall look in them in vain for any trace of venom towards the General Council or towards Marx." Bakunin preserved so keen a sense of justice and so splendid a magnanimity, that on January 28, 1872, writing to the internationalists of the Romagna about Marx and the Marxists, he said:—

"Fortunately for the International, there existed in London a group of men who were extremely devoted to the great association and who were, in the true sense of the words, the real founders and initiators of that body. I speak of the small group of Germans whose leader is Karl Marx. These estimable persons regard me as an enemy, and maltreat me as such whenever and wherever they can. They are greatly mistaken. I am in no respect their enemy, and it gives me, on the contrary, lively satisfaction when I am able to do them justice. I often have an opportunity of doing so, for I regard them as genuinely important and worthy persons, in respect both of intelligence and knowledge, and also in respect of their passionate devotion to the cause of the proletariat and of a loyalty to that cause which has withstood every possible test—a devotion and a loyalty which have been proved by the achievements of twenty years. Marx is the supreme economic and socialist genius of our day. In the course of my life, I have come into contact with a great many learned men, but I know no one else who is so profoundly learned as he. Engels, who is now secretary for Italy and Spain, Marx's friend and pupil, is also a man of outstanding intelligence. As long ago as 1846 and 1848, working together, they founded the Party of the German Communists, and their activities in this direction have continued ever since. Marx edited the profound and admirable Preamble to the Provisional Rules of the International and gave a body to the instinctively unanimous aspirations of the proletariat of nearly all countries of Europe, in that, during the years 1863-1864 he conceived the idea of the International and effected its establishment. These are great and splendid services, and it would be very ungrateful of us if we were reluctant to acknowledge their importance."

Bakunin explains the breach between Marx and himself:—

"Marx is an authoritarian and centralising communist. He wants what we want, the complete triumph of economic and social equality, but he wants it in the State and through the State power, through the dictatorship of a very strong and, so to say, despotic provisional government, that is, by the negation of liberty. His economic ideal is the State as sole owner of the land and of all kinds of capital, cultivating the land through well-paid agricultural association under the management of State engineers, and controlling all industrial and commercial associations with State capital.

"We want the same triumph of economic and social equality through the abolition of the State, and of all that passes by the name of law (which, in our view, is the permanent negation of human rights). We want the reconstruction of society, and the unification of mankind, to be achieved, not from above downwards, by any sort of authority, or by socialist officials, engineers, and other accredited men of learning—but from below upwards, by the free federation of all kinds of workers' associations liberated from the yoke of the State.

"You see that two theories could hardly be more sharply opposed to one another than are ours. But there is another difference between us, a purely personal one.

"Marx has two odious faults: he is vain and jealous. He detested Proudhon, simply because Proudhon's great name and well-deserved reputation were prejudicial to him. There is no term of abuse that Marx has failed to apply to Proudhon. Marx is egotistical to the pitch of insanity. He talks of 'my ideas,' and cannot understand that ideas belong to no one in particular, but that, if we look carefully, we shall always find that the best and greatest ideas are the product of the instinctive labour of all..... Marx, who was already constitutionally inclined towards selfglorification, was definitely corrupted by the idolisation of his disciples, who have made a sort of doctrinaire pope out of him. Nothing can be more disastrous to the mental and moral health of a man even though he be extremely intelligent, than to be idolised and regarded as infallible. All this has made Marx even more egotistical, so that he is beginning to loathe every one who will not bow the neck before him."

Ruhle had dealt very exhaustively with the steps taken by Marx to get rid of his hated adversary. Marx organised irregular conferences at London and the Hague. Bakunin, Guillaume, and Schuizgulbed were expelled by methods since employed by the Third International to expel Trotskyists and other opponents of present day Stalinism. The Purge was always a characteristic of Marxism. A victory was won that secured not fruit. Marx had to admit that the last Congress of the International, held at Geneva, in September, 1873, was a complete fiasco. Becker wrote a letter to Serge describing Marx's hopeless intrigues in connection with this Congress.

Marx decided to throw a last handful of mud at Bakunin. With Engels and Lafargue, he undertook to publish a report of the charges made against Bakunin, under the title "Die Allianz Der Sozialistisch en Demokratie Und Die International Arbeitassoziation". (The Alliance of the socialist Democracy and the International Working Men's Association), Every line of this report is a distortion, every allegation an injustice, every argument a falsification and every word an untruth. As Ruhle says, even Mehring although so indulgent to Marx places this work "at the lowest rank" among all those published by Marx and Engels.

Bakunin met the attack with resignation. He described the pamphlet as a "gendarme denunciation." He declared that Marx, urged onwards by furious hatred, had undertaken to expose himself before the public in the role of a sneaking and calumniatory police agent.

Bakunin added :—

"That is his own affair ; and, since he likes the job, let him have it ...... This has given me an intense loathing of public life. I have had enough of it. I therefore withdraw from the arena, and ask only one thing from my dear contemporaries—oblivion."

When Bakunin died, on July 1, 1876, no trace of the Marxian International remained.

Marxism degenerated into the 2nd International, parliamentary opportunism and careerism, and the Nationalistic support of the First Great War. After that war, it gave us the machinations of the 3rd International, the assassination of Socialists and Socialism in Soviet Russia; the debacle in Germany, the betrayal in Spain leading to the triumph of Fascism; and, finally, the dictatorship diplomacy which released the Second Great War by signing a pact with Germany : the great Stalin-Hitler alliance, the Soviet-Nazi pact. Marxism is dead; and the world of libertian struggle recalls the wisdom and the defiance of Bakunin. Marx is dead and Bakunin strides on, leading the workers of the world on to the conquest of bread and freedom—and roses too. To-day, the name of Bakunin is lined historically and traditionally with the emancipation of the human race. In death, he is symbol of anti-Fascism. He is legend, power, and reality.

APPENDIX IV.

UNLIKE Proudhon or Marx, the two other great radical figures of his time, Michael Bakunin, characterised by none other than Peter Kropotkin as the founder of modern anarchism, never bequeathed to his followers a more or less systematic body of ideas; indeed, it was Kropotkin himself who, drawing on his extensive reading and scientific training, established the principles of the anarchist movement of to-day. However, what Bakunin did was of no trifling nature: fragments of theory, inspired orations and letters of gargantuan length helped spread anarchism throughout Europe. Even more important perhaps was the example of his life, a life which, in the words of Otto Ruhle, the biographer of Marx, marked him as "one of the most brilliant, heroic and fascinating of revolutionsists the world has ever known."

As a child Bakunin received a liberal education from his father and tutors, who were guided by the precepts of Rousseau's *Emile,* but in 1852, after the death of Alexander I, the Decembrist uprising took place in Petersburg, and the elderly landowner, frightened at the reaction which followed, sought to dispel dangerous ideas from his son's mind by enrolling him in the Tsar's Artillery School. Young Michael finally gained a commission though he had shown little interest for military studies and had spent most of the time writing long letters home trying to counteract parental authority over his brothers and sisters. At this time, soon after he had found a way to abandon his military career, he became initiated into the young intellectual circles of Moscow and fell under the spell of Fichte and Hegel, the reigning German gods of Russian romanticism. Bakunin, in this stage of his development, has been described by a friend, Vissarion Belinsky, later the conservative critic, in adjectives which were always to fit: "Strength, undisciplined power, unquiet, excitable, deep-seated spiritual unrest, incessant striving for some distant goal, dissatisfaction with the present." Such a person could not but find it impossible to breathe freely in the stagnating atmosphere of Russian feudalism, so, in 1840, with the consent of his father who had finally given up all hope of his son settling down to a respectable oblivion, Bakunin departed for Berlin to court the Hegelian system at its source.

First Essay

Under the spell still of orthodox Hegelianism, flying the banner of philosophical reaction: "That which is rational is real, and that which is real is rational", Bakunin had not yet changed intellectually from being anything but a loyal subject of the Tsar. In his sub-conscious, though, he had broken with his traditions, and the breach was furthered consciously by the materialist thought of the Left Hegelians. It was under the influence of Strauss and Feuerbach that Bakunin wrote his first important essay, *Reaction in Germany*, with its uncompromising view of reality: "The Left say 'Two and two are four; the Right say 'Two and two are six'; and the juste milieu says 'Two and two are five." This essay also contained the famous phrase, "The urge for destruction is also a creative urge", which was later seized on by his enemies and misinterpreted to slander him as a creature with a sadistic urge for mere destruction.

By the phrase Bakunin meant that the old corrupt society must first be done away with before we can achieve the new. The so-called Apostle of Destruction added on more than one occasion, as George Woodcock has pointed out, "Bloody revolutions are often necessary, thanks to human stupidity; yet they are always an evil, a monstrous evil and a great disaster, not only with regard to the victims, but also for the sake of the purity and perfection of the purpose in whose name they take place."

In 1843 his intellectual flight into radicalism became physically pressing, and he left Germany for Switzerland where he made the acquaintance of Wilhelm Weitling, an authoritarian communist, who had somewhat inconsistently written in his book *Guarantees of Harmony and Freedom,* this harbinger of Bakunin's future view: "The perfect society has no government, but only an administration, no laws, but only obligations, no punishments, but means of correction". This association was short-lived, however, for Weitling was arrested for stepping on the religious beliefs of the Swiss burghers, and when Bakunin's name was found among the prisoner's papers, the Russian scarcely had time to elude the police. But they had contacted the authorities in Russia, and when Bakunin refused to obey a call to return home, he was condemned in absence to a loss of his inheritance and exile to Siberia, a sentence which Tsar Nicholas would carry out, with a vengeance, some ten years later.

Meets Marx and Proudhon

Paris was Bakunin's next restless resting-place, and there he brought his worldly possessions of a single trunk, a folding and a zinc wash-basin, relying for funds on teaching, translations from the German and like many revolutionists of his time and some of ours, on liberal loans from grumbling friends. In Paris Bakunin's anarchist ideas began fermenting as he came in contact with George Sand, Pierre Leroux, Considerant, the leader of the Fourierists, and attended meetings of French working-men. But it was two others he met whose influence was to be more decisive—Pierre-Joseph Proudhon and Karl Marx, the resolute the centralist, and Bakunin, already a believer in direct action, clashed immediately. "He called me a sentimental idealist," said Bakunin later, "and he was right; I called him gloomy, unreliable and vain, and I was right too." And elsewhere Bakunin had said: "Marx is carrying on the same sort of futile activities as of old, corrupting the workers by making them argumentative." However, this dislike for the tactics and character of Marx, whose domineering attitude was in time to be instrumental in wrecking the forces of socialism, did not blind Bakunin to his merits: "At this time I understood nothing of political economy, and my socialism was purely instinctive. He, though he was younger than I, was an atheist, an instructed materialist, and a conscious socialist." His meetings with Proudhon were more congenial and resulted in a mutual influence with Bakunin introducing the French master to Hegel and others. "Yet despite these substantial obligations," writes E. H. Carr in his generally barren biography of Bakunin, "Bakunin in later years always spoke of his debt to Proudhon, never of Proudhon's debt to him."

Direct Action

1848 was a year of decision for Bakunin just as it was in the life of Europe. In February a revolution had broken out in France against Louis-Philippe, and soon Bakunin was in the thick of it and in the hair of the new authorities. This was the first actual contact the veteran of revolution had made with an uprising, and, as he wrote, never had he found anywhere "such noble self-sacrifice, such a touching sense of honour, so much natural delicacy of behaviour, so much friendly gaiety combined with so much heroism, as among these simple uneducated people." He left no account of his own activities, but Caussidiere, the revolutionary Prefect of Police, is said to have exclaimed: "What a man! In the first day of a revolution he is a perfect treasure; on the second, he ought to be shot." And Flocon said: "If there were three hundred Bakunins, it would be impossible to govern France." It is not surprising that the French authorities gave Bakunin permission to leave the country when seeing that the Europe established by the Congress of Vienna was tottering, he sought to spread the message of revolution elsewhere. The next year found him aiding the Polish insurrection, fighting on the barricades with Czech students and participating in the Dresden uprising where he met Richard Wagner, then a revolutionist, who later, according to Bernard Shaw, used Bakunin as the model for the Siegfried of music dramas.

Prison and Exile

When Bakunin appeared in London more than twelve years later, such friends as Alexander Herzen, the famous Russian liberal, might have mistaken him for a ghost except that spirits were not supposed to be so massive in their build and so eloquent on the subject of materialism. He had spent eight years in the dungeons of four countries, handed about like some curious monster on exhibit, and then four years of Siberian exile; years of equal torture to his robust body and vigorous mind, days of depression and nights of sleeplessness, all so demoralizing that when he was handed over to the Russian authorities and buried alive in the infamous Peter-and-Paul fortress (which later was to 'lodge' Kropotkin), he penned—at the suggestion of the Tsar—his Confession, a document of dostoievskian self-abasement, which was to be made public by the Bolsheviks in 1921 and which Bakunin himself, in his correspondence, considered 'a great blunder'.

A True Seeker

The years after imprisonment and exile found Bakunin becoming more and more a conscious anarchist though never in any sense of dull dogmatism, for as he put it: "No theory, no ready-made system, no book that has ever been written will save the world. I cleave to no system, I am a true seeker." That does not mean, though, that Bakunin had no radical moorings: he had come to realize after his relations with Continental uprisings that nationalist movements could not bring about the social revolution; that, going beyond Marx in his materialist interpretation of capitalist society, the State could become a ruling class above the existing capitalistic rulers, and that in the place of both must come the expropriation of land and the means of production to be worked collectively by workers' associations. With these views taking shape, Bakunin began to realize, too, that what was needed for its accomplishment was an international revolutionary movement. For a time he worked within the radical democratic organization, the League for Peace and Freedom, building a reputation as an orator and gaining numbers of adherents to his ideas, notably the brothers

Elisee and Elie Reclus. But it was not long before Bakunin became disgusted with the essentially bourgeois nature of the League and founded his International Alliance of Social Democracy which soon gained, with the help of spirited Bakounian letters (the pharse is vanzetti's), thousands of followers in Switzerland, Italy and Spain. In 1868 Bakunin had joined the International Working Men's Association and he soon saw that it was foolish to divide the forces of labour by maintaining his own organization and, therefore, after petitioning the General Council, led by Marx, he was allowed to enter the Alliance into the International though only as separate branches. Marx already considered Bakunin as a menace to his own authority.

The proceedings of the International after Bakunin's entry are fraught with prophetic significance for the radical movement of to-day; it left us a heritage of radical watchwords, realised by the workers themselves, which are still vital now, but, unfortunately, it also left a sorry legacy of dirty tactics, involving slander, contrived voting and purges, which have all but ruined the socialist movements which followed. Even Franz Mehring and Otto Ruhle, the admiring biographers of Marx, have been forced to put the blame for what developed on their master's shoulders.

Struggle in the International

However, it is wrong to believe that it was principally petty politics and character differences which caused the monumental clash between Marx and Bakunin. In his last years, for his death was near, Bakunin examined the real issues at stake in a letter to the Internationalists of Romagna which is worth quoting at length. He was able to say despite all the calumny: "Fortunately for the International there existed in London a group of men who were, in the true sense of the words, the real founders and initiators of that body. I speak of the small group of Germans whose leader is Karl Marx. These estimable persons regard me as an enemy, and maltreat me as such whenever and wherever they can. They are greatly mistaken. I am in no respect their enemy and it gives me on the contrary lively satisfaction when I am able to do them justice. I have often an opportunity of doing so, for I regard them as genuinely important and estimable persons, in respect both of intelligence and knowledge, and also in respect of their passionate devotion to the cause of the proletariat and of a loyalty to that cause which has withstood every possible test—a devotion and a loyalty which has been proved by the achievements of twenty years. Marx is the supreme economic and socialist genius of our day. In the course of my life, I have come in contact with a great many learned men, but I know no one else who is so profoundly learned as he. Engels, who is now secretary for Italy and Spain, Marx's friend and pupil, is also a man of outstanding intelligence. As long ago as 1846 and 1848, working together, they founded the party of the German communists, and their activities in this direction have continued ever since. Marx edited the profound and admirable Preamble to the Provisional Rules of the International, and gave a body to the instinctively unanimous aspirations of the proletariat of nearly all countries of Europe, in that, during the years 1863-1864 he conceived the International and affected its establishment. These are great and splendid services, and it would be very ungrateful of us if we were reluctant to acknowledge their importance." Then why the clash? Bakunin goes on: Marx is an authoritarian and centralizing communist. He wants what we want: the complete triumph of economic and social equality, but he wants it in the State and through the State power, the dictatorship of a very strong and, so to say, despotic provisional government, that is, by the negation of liberty. His economic ideal is the State as sole owner of the land and of all kinds of capital, cultivating the land through well-paid agricultural associations under the management of State engineers, and controling all industrial and commercial enterprises with State capital.

"We want the same triumph of economic and social equality throught the abolition of the State, and of all that passes by the name of law (which, in our view, is the permanent negation of human rights). We want a reconstruction of society, and the unification of mankind, to be achieved, not from above downwards, by any sort of authority, or by socialist officials, engineers, and other accredited men of learning—but from below upwards, by the free federation of all kinds of workers' associations liberated from the yoke of the State.

"You see that two theories could hardly be more sharply opposed to one another than ours are. But there is another difference between us, a purely personal one.

"Marx has two odious faults: he is vain and jealous. He detested Proudhon, simply because Proudhon's great name and well-deserved reputation were prejudicial to him. There is no term of abuse that Marx failed to apply to Proudhon. Marx is egotistical to the pitch of insanity. He talks of 'my ideas', and cannot understand that ideas belong to no one in particular, but that, if we look very carefully, we shall always find that the best and greatest ideas are the product of the instinctive labour of all......"

Bakunin saw the struggle clearly but after his expulsion from the International, his strength began to decline rapidly. He started but failed to complete several theoritical works, notably *The State Idea and Anarchy* and *The Knouto-Germanic Empire*, a document full of insights into what later developed into Nazism. He further saw the shape of the future in one of his last letters, when, despairing over the defeat of the Paris Commune and the reaction that followed, he wrote to Elisee Reclus: "There remains another hope, the world war. Sooner or later these enormous military states will have to destroy and devour each other. But what an outlook!" On July 1st 1876, he died in Berne, and overcautious Swiss followers, when asked by the police what the deceased's occupation or means of livelihood had been, replied that he had been the owner of a villa in Italian Switzerland. The police listed the dead man in the official records as "Michel de Bakounine, rentier."

Michael Bakunin's place in the company of great anarchists of the past has been based, in the seventy years since his death, more on the spirit of his personality than on the substance of his mind. This is especially so in the English-speaking world where his *God and the State* now reprinted, has been the only complete fragment (so to speak) translated. And it is true that Bakunin never had the socratic skill of Proudhon; Godwin was far his superior when it came to formal reason as Kropotkin was in the matter of scientific method, and he certainly did not possess the keen common sense of a Malatesta.

Bakunin's Influence

But it is wrong to assume that Bakunin was merely (the noun belongs to Marx) an unusual "bullock" in the revolutionary arena.

Some might say to-day, as E. H. Carr does, that Bakunin's personality was distinctly neurotic. That does not lessen the part he played in founding the revolutionary anarchist movement in Europe, especially in Spain where, during the Revolution of 1936, many of the anarchist ideas proved their practical value.

Nor does the term "neurotic." or his inferiority in the company of those more dialectically skilled dull his insights into the problem of achieving a just and free world. It is as though we were listening to a man still alive, commenting on an international conference, when we read: "It would be a fearful contradiction and absurd naivete on our part to express, as has been done at the present Congress [Bakunin was speaking before the League for Peace and Freedom], the desire to establish international justice, freedom, and peace, and at the same time wish to retain the State. States cannot be made to change their nature, since it is in virtue of that they *are* States, and if they renounce it, they cease to exist. There cannot therefore be a good, just, and moral State. All States are bad in the sense that they constitute by their nature, *i. e.*, by the conditions of the porpose for which they exist, the absolute negation of human justice, freedom and morality. And in this respect, whatever you may say,- there is no great difference between the uncouth Russian Empire and the most civilized States of Europe. The Tsarist Empire [read Stalinist] does cynically what other States do under the mask of hypocrisy; it represents, in its open, despotic, contemptuous attitude to humanity, the secret ideal which is the aim and delight of all European statesmen and officials. All European States [and we might add those of other continents] do what they are doing insofar as they are not prevented by public opinion and, in particular, by the new but already powerful solidarity of the working classes, which carries in itself the seed of the destruction of the State. Only a weak State can be a virtuous State, and even it is wicked in its thoughts and its desires."

Or litsen to Bakunin in these words, a possible inspiration for Kropotkin's *Mutual Aid*: "Man becomes man, and his humanity becomes conscious and real, only in society and by the joint activity of society. He frees himself from the yoke of external nature only by joint—that is, societary—labour; it alone is capable of making the surface of the earth fit for the evolution of mankind; but without such external liberation neither intellectual nor moral liberation is possible . . . Outside of society man would have remained forever a wild beast, or, what comes to about the same thing, a saint. Finaly, in his isolation man cannot have the consciousness of liberty. What liberty means for man is that he is recognized as free, and treated as free, by those who surround him; liberty is not a matter of isolation, therefore, but of mutuality—not of separateness, but of combination; for every man it is only the mirroring of his humanity (that is, of his human rights) in the consciousness of his brothers.

Bakunin's place in all this? Let him speak for himself: "You tell me [he wrote to a correspondent] that I can become the Garibaldi of socialism? I care very little to become a Garibaldi and play a grotesque role. I shall die and the worms will eat me, but I want our idea to triumph. I want the masses of humanity to be really emancipated from all authorities and from all heroes present, and to come."

(MICHAEL GRIEG ON BAKUNIN.)

SOCIALISM AND STATE

WITH A SHORT BIOGRAPHY OF RUDOLF ROCKER

In this brochure:-

Socialism & its various tendencies: Influence of democratic & liberal ideas on the socialist movement: Babouvism & Jacobinism: Caesaristic & Theocratic ideas in socialism: Proudhon and Federalism: International Workingmen's Association: Bakunin opposed to the central state power: The Paris Commune & its influence on the socialist movement: Parliamentary activity and the International: Franco-Prussian war and the political change in Europe: The modern labour parties and the struggle for power: Socialism and National politics: Authoritarian and liberal socialism: Government or administration.

Price 6 annas.

ANARCHO-SYNDICALISM

By
RUDOLF ROCKER

The author traces the history of the origin, growth and the present conditions of the Anarchist movement, unfolds the principles of labour organisation from anarchist point of view and brings out the essential difference between Trade Unionism & Anarchist Syndicalism. Here is the book that every man and woman, interested in labour politics, should buy & read.

Price Rs. 2/8

READ !   READ !!

"FREEDOM"   "WORD"

Journals of Anarchism in the West

Annas 3 inclusive of postage. Sample copy free.

Obtainable at:—
    LIBERTARIAN BOOK HOUSE,
    Arya Bhavan, Sandhurst Road,
    Bombay, 4.

"ANARCHISM IS THE FUTURE
ORDER OF THE DAY."

ROOT IS MAN

or

PROGRESSIVISM *versus* **RADICALISM?**

Principal contents of the book.

(1) We need a new Political Vocabulary.

(2) The World We Live In.

(3) What is Marxism?

(4) Mirage of Proletarean Revolution.

(5) Bureaucratic Collectivism.

(6) Modern War and Class Struggle.

(7) Marxism and Value.

(8) Idea of Progress.

(9) Towards a New Concept of Political Action.

Etc.

Do not fail to read this Book written by once a Communist Dwight Macdonald. Price Rs. 2

Obtainable from:—
      LIBERTARIAN BOOK HOUSE,
   Arya Bhavan, Sandhurst Road, Bombay, 4.

SOME CONTENTS OF
WHAT IS MUTUALISM?
BY SWARTZ.

MUTUALISM—A Social System Based on Equal Freedom, Reciprocity and the Sovereignty of the Individual Over Himself, His Affairs, and His Products, Realized Through Individual Initiative, Free Contract, Co-operation, Competition, and Voluntary Association for Defence Against the Invasive and for the Protection of Life, Liberty and Property of the Non-Invasive.

PRINCIPAL CONTENTS.

The Growth of Monopoly, The State as Oppressor, Nefarious Features of Present System, Socialism, The Single Tax.

Mutualism Universally Applicable, The four Great Monopolies, Co-operation and Competition.

What is Money? The Gold Monopoly, The Profits of Banking. What is interest? Power of interest, Price Level theory Awkward, Not more but More flexible Currency Needed. Value of paper Money, Necessity for Sound Basis for Money. What is Credit? Insurance of Credit, The Mutual Bank, The Marginal Producer Benefit to Farmer and Manufacturer, Benefit to the Wage Worker.

The Constitution of Price, Patents and Copyright, Semi-Public Service Enteprise under Mutualism.

Tendency to Evade Taxes, Voluntary Association Organised Labor's Opportunity. To do away with the Monopolies of Land and Money.

Pages 250   Price 3-8-0.

Obtainable at :—
LIBERTARIAN BOOK HOUSE,
ARYA BHAVAN, SANDHURST ROAD,
BOMBAY, 4.
OR
MODERN PUBLISHERS, INDORE CITY.

THE BOOK THAT YOU MUST READ
(Write for your copy to-day)

GOD AND THE STATE

By Michael Bakunin.

Pages 106, Price Rs. 2/-

Communalism is the deadliest poison in the body politic of India today. Not a day passes when innocent men, women and even children do not die of the so-called religious warfare. It is strange to see the touching and pathetic appeals seemingly emerging from the very core of the hearts of the top-ranking leaders go unheeded. : not a minute's thought is given to the naked fact that stares in the face of every Indian that this religious and communal fanatical tension is withholding the dawn of liberty, making the four hundred million people a mere laughing stock for the civilised world.

Obviously something is fundamentally wrong somewhere. Experience has shown that mere verbal appeals will not help. What is needed is proper understanding by the masses as to what exactly religion is and what possible connection it can have with the state. The well-wishers of India would do no better than to read "GOD AND THE STATE" wherein MICHAEL BAKUNIN, a contemporary of Karl Marx, prominent figure in the First International, has located the place of religion in human life and its relation with the state. Written with a cool, calm and calculating mind, the book deserves study.

Can be had from
**Libertarian Book House,
Arya Bhavan,
Sandhurst Road, Bombay, 4.**

Have You Read?

NATIONALISM AND CULTURE

By : Rudolf Rocker.

..........................Perhaps Not.

SEE!

What Those Who Have Read It, Say About The Book:-

From a Leader in Social Progress:

A BOOK OF TREMENDOUS VALUE

Thank you for the copy of "Nationalism and Culture" by Rudolf Rocker. I have already begun reading the book and am impressed by its philosophical soundness. I have examined the book and have read far enough to be able to give you my impression. I think Mr. Rocker has written a book of tremendous value. It is most opportune, coming as it does at this period of the world's history when the domination of force is so highly manifested.

The expansion of centralized power vested in political governments is the great disaster threatening the world at the present time. Wars, the ardent brutalities, and social disorganization which they engender are the natural result of such politically centralized force. Mr. Rocker, in his "Nationalism and Culture," philosophically evaluates the significance of these forces. I hope this book may be widely read. It is much needed.

J. P. Warbasse,
President,
The Cooperative League,
167 W. 12th St., N. Y.

BOOKS THAT ALL SHOULD READ

NATIONALISM AND CULTURE by Rudolf Roker ...
SYNOPOSIS OF NATIONALISM AND CULTURE ..
WHAT IS MUTUALISM ? by Swartz
PARSPARVAD (GUJERATI) by Swartz
MUTUAL BANKING by Green
A.B.C. OF ANARCHISM by Berkman
COMMUNISM by Guy Aldred
ANARCHY by Malatesta
GOD AND THE STATE by Michael Bakunin
SOCIALISM AND STATE by Rudolf Rocker
WAGE SYSTEM by Peter Kropotkin
ANARCHISM IN SOCIALIST EVOLUTION
        by Peter Kropotkin ...
TRADE UNIONISM or SYNDICALISM ..
STATE & ITS HISTORIC ROLE by Peter Kropotkin ..
ANARCHO-SYNDICALISM by Rudolf Rocker ..
DOES GOD EXIST? by Sebastien Faure
REBUILDING THE WORLD
      by John Beverley Robinson
SOCIAL DEMOCRACY VERSUS COMMUNISM
        by Karl Kautsky ...
ROADS TO FREEDOM by Bertrand Russel .
GENERAL IDEA OF THE REVOLUTION IN THE
   19th CENTURY by Proudhon ..
OUR ECONOMIC PROBLEMS by Pro J.f. D. Unwin ...
ROOT IS MAN (PROGRESSIVISM VS.
   RADICALISM) by Dwight Macdonald
ECONOMICS OF LIBERTY by J. Beverly Robinson
WHAT IS COOPERATION by P. Warbasse
        (bound in cloth & cardboard ...

Available at:—

LIBERTARIAN BOOK HOUSE

Arya Bhavan, Sandhurst Road, BOMBAY 4

&

Modern Publishers, INDORE.

**PLEASE DO NOT REMOVE
CARDS OR SLIPS FROM THIS POCKET**

UNIVERSITY OF TORONTO LIBRARY

HX
915
B155

Bakunin, Mikhail
Aleksandrovich
   Bakunin's Writings

SD - #0040 - 280922 - C0 - 229/152/7 - PB - 9781332608737 - Gloss Lamination